A Handbook of Mystical Theology

THE IBIS WESTERN MYSTERY TRADITION SERIES

The heritage of all Western spirituality, both open and esoteric, and all the systems, theories, and practices that relate to it, are drawn from a single source: the Judeao-Christian spiritual tradition. This tradition has yet deeper roots in the distinctive religious faiths of the great civilzations of Egypt, Greece, and Mesopotamia.

At the heart of all these great traditions lies their ultimate goal: the spiritual regeneration of humanity. There is more than one Way to its attainment, and it is the totality of the many paths that lead us back to our primal source that constitutes the Western Mystery Tradition. They are encapsulated in the countless texts that enshrine and reflect the work of the inspired men and women who have dedicated their lives to preserving, interpreting, and transmitting this tradition.

Many of these text have become a part of the canon of Western literature, but there are many others that have been unjustly neglected, hidden in times of persecution, or have simply gone unrecognized. Some record exalted inner experiences, some are guides to esoteric practice, while others are speculative studies of esoteric knowledge and spiritual wisdom. All of them have one feature in common: an inherent power to enrich us spiritually.

It is from rare printed versions of these unknown or forgotten texts, and from studies of them, that the Ibis series of classics of the Western Mystery Tradition is drawn.

—The Editors of Ibis Press

A
Handbook
of
Mystical Theology

G. B. Scaramelli, S. J.

Translated
by
D.H.S. Nicholson

Introduction by
Allan Armstrong

Ibis Press
An Imprint of Nicolas-Hays, Inc.
Berwick, Maine

This edition published in 2005 by
Ibis Press, an imprint of
Nicolas-Hays, Inc.
P. O. Box 1126
Berwick, ME 03901-1126
www.nicolashays.com
First published in London in 1913 by John Watkins

Distributed to the trade by
Red Wheel/Weiser, LLC
P. O. Box 612
York Beach, ME 03910-0612
www.redwheelweiser.com

Library of Congress Cataloging-in-Publication Data
available by request

Cover design by Kathryn Sky-Peck.
Printed in the United States of America

11	10	09	08	07	06	05
7	6	5	4	3	2	1

VG

The paper used in this publication meets the
minimum requirements of the American National
Standard for Information Sciences—Permanence
of Paper for Printed Library Materials Z39.48–1992
(R1997).

INTRODUCTION

Giovanni Battista Scaramelli was born in Rome in 1687. In 1706, when he was almost 19 years old, he entered the Society of Jesus, where he remained for the rest of his life. He died in 1752, at Macerata, a provincial city of central Italy lying between the Chienti and the Potenza rivers. Little is known about his personal life, except what may be inferred from his written works. What is known is that on becoming a Jesuit, and presumably after serving his noviciate, he devoted himself to preaching for the following fifteen years. Examining what it is to be a Jesuit may help us understand the character of a man whose entire adult life was shaped by The Society of Jesus.

The Society was founded by the Spanish mystic, Ignatius of Loyola, in 1540. It is a mendicant order of what are termed "clerks regular," which is a body of priests, organized for apostolic work, that follows a religious rule and relies on alms for its support. Since its inception, the Society's main objective has been the propagation and strengthening of the Catholic faith, and the Jesuits' missionary ambitions were directed toward non-Christian lands such as India, Japan, China, and the Americas. Members of the Society differ from other religious orders in that as well as taking upon themselves the vows of poverty, chastity, and obedience, they are bound by a fourth vow of complete obedience to the will of the pope in matters spiritual, even unto death. This vow has ever set them apart from other monastic orders, and has earned them the reputation of being the "secret service" of the Roman Catholic Church, and are generally recognized as being the main instruments of the Counter-Reformation.

The Society's constitution, drawn up by Ignatius, has never been altered. The chief authority is vested in the superior general,[1] who is elected for life, and who invariably resides in Rome. His authority is supreme, although every member of the Society has the right to a private communication with him. The order is divided into provinces, each province governed by a provincial, who is appointed by the superior general. The provincial is responsible for the appointment of local superiors, with the exception of the rectors of colleges, provosts of professed houses, and masters of novices, who are appointed by the superior general. Provincials and rectors of colleges usually hold office for no more than three years.

Members of the society fall into the following classes: novices, temporal coadjutors, scholastics, spiritual coadjutors, and professed fathers. The novitiate lasts two years, at the end of which novices take the simple vows of the regulars—chastity, poverty, and obedience—and join the ranks of the temporal coadjutors. Those aspiring to the priesthood become scholastics, remaining in this grade for a further fifteen years or so, in which time they will complete their studies, spend a period of time teaching, and receive their ordination to the priesthood. At the end of this time the scholastic will complete another year of spiritual training known as the tertianship,

---

[1] Sometimes given the derogatory title of "the Black Pope."

after which he will become a spiritual coadjutor. If he is to become professed he will make his vows of chastity, poverty, and obedience solemn vows, and add an additional solemn vow to obey the pope in all matters spiritual, undertaking to go wherever he may be sent, without, so it is said, "even requiring money for the journey." The "professed of the four vows" constitute the core of the Society, the other grades being regarded as probationary and terminable.

At the heart of the Society lies the *Spiritual Exercises*, which were developed by Ignatius of Loyola himself on the basis of his many years' experience in ascetic and mystical endeavor. They were primarily intended for the Society members' use, under the supervision of a spiritual director, and were never intended for popular use, although today they are commonly available. Indeed, it is a fundamental part of the novitiate that novices enter into retreat for a period of thirty days to be guided through the *Spiritual Exercises*. This retreat is an important test of the novices' vocation as the life and activity of the Society are built around these exercises, and are undoubtedly a key factor in forming the Jesuit character. Consequently, in accordance with the ideals and concepts presented in the *Spiritual Exercises*, the novice is trained in a meditative approach to the study of the truths and principles of faith, in the discipline of self-examination, and in the education and sublimation of personal will, which the novice offers to the service of God, following the divine will of Christ as revealed through His appointed authorities here on earth. This is what is meant by

Jesuit obedience, which is the distinctive virtue of the Society—respecting authority and complying with its decisions with the conviction that as best can be ascertained, such decisions express, for the time, the will of God.

That he was a Jesuit and committed defender of the Catholic church is a matter of fact, but Scaramelli was also a mystic, perhaps less well-known than he should be, yet still a mystic, whose spiritual life was not only deeply influenced by the teachings of the Society of Jesus but also by the teachings of many of the saints of the Church, such as St. Teresa d'Avila and St. John of the Cross, who were both influenced by those who went before: St. John of the Cross was conversant with the works of the Pseudo-Dionysius and many of the medieval mystics, and quotes freely from them.

Scaramelli's written works emerged late in his life. He wrote five books in all, of which only two were published in his lifetime.[2] His most important work, *Il direttorio mistico*, was published posthumously at

[2] *Vita di Suor Maria Crocifissa Satellico Monaca francescana nel monastero di monte Nuovo,* was published in Venice, 1750, the *Direttorio ascetico in cui s'insegna il modo di condurre l'Anime per vie ordinarie della grazia alla perfezione christiana, indirizzato ai direttori della Anime* was published in Naples, 1752. The *Discernimento de' spiriti per il retto regolamento delle azione proprie ed altrui Operetta utile specialemente ai Direttori delle anime,* was published posthumously in 1753, as was *Il direttorio mistico indrizato a' direttori di quelle anime che Iddio conduce per la via della contemplazione,* published Venice 1754; *Dottrina di S. Giovanni della Croce compresa quali si contiene la 'Salita del Monte', nel secondo le 'Notti oscue', nel terzo 'l'Esercizio di Amore' e la 'Fiamma di Amor vivo,* published Lucca, 1860.

Venice in 1754. It is this title of which *The Handbook of Mystical Theology* is an abridged translation.

Scaramelli divided *The Handbook of Mystical Theology* into five books. In the first book, he introduces the reader to medieval psychology as defined in the writings of the Scholastics, particularly Thomas Aquinas. It is a psychology that was steadfastly adhered to by the Catholic church until recent times and in many ways it still has its supporters. Humanity, Scaramelli states, is composed of two parts; the rational part and the physical, or biological, part. The rational part consists of the intellect, the memory, and the will, by which we perform spiritual actions. To the physical part are attributed the exterior and interior senses, by which we experience life in its various natural dimensions. Although his physics may now be redundant, his outline of human experience has much to offer the spiritual aspirant of today.

He closes the first book by introducing the reader to the sublime notion that the beginning of mystical experience is not simply the result of human initiative but the influx of spiritual power in the form of two kinds of grace: Sanctifying Grace, by which we receive the spiritual power to enter upon the spiritual path, and Actual Grace, which consists of an illumination of the intellect that motivates the will and arouses the soul to action, infusing it with the gifts of the Holy Spirit. In his description of Sanctifying Grace there can be seen the subtle influence of the Blessed Jan van Ruysbroeck, who taught that the spiritual life is not simply a matter of the soul rejecting the world and turning to God; rather, if it is to succeed in its spiritual endeavors, then it is essential that the light of divine grace touch the soul and quicken it. Ruysbroeck describes this quickening grace as the "Prevenient Grace" of God, which prepares the soul for the reception of another higher light of divine grace—an inward and mysterious working of God that moves the soul and all its powers.[3] It is the work of this grace, a work described by Scaramelli as "Actual Grace," that enables the soul to continue in the spiritual work through developing the virtues of faith and charity, thereby preparing the soul for the influx of the gifts of the Holy Spirit.

In the second book, Scaramelli introduces the reader to the disciplines of meditation and contemplation, and discusses the relationship between them. As far as he is concerned, meditation is a laborious, but necessary discipline of discursive reasoning that leads the soul to the point where it may enter into contemplation. He cautions the reader that it is a grave mistake to attempt contemplation before the time is ripe, for the attainment of contemplation must be preceded by meditation. It is not a question of choice between one and the other but a process of growth from meditation into contemplation. In this he echoes the teachings of the Pseudo-Dionysius who taught that before we can transcend the limitations of our own nature we must first see it for what it is: then, and only then, may we set about the task of transcending it. Furthermore, like Dionysius,

---

[3] See *The Adornment of the Spiritual Marriage with The Book of Truth & The Sparkling Stone*, C. A. Wynschenk Dom, trans. (Berwick, ME: Ibis Press, 2005).

he shows us how, through contemplation, we may advance from being instinctive creatures whose understanding is determined by sensory experience, to being rational creatures whose understanding is enhanced by the transformative power of the grace of God and drawn into the indescribable unity that we intuitively know to be the source, ground, and cause of all life.

Scaramelli describes meditation as a discipline that involves directing the faculties of the mind to the purpose of shaping our nature according to the will of God. In this he reminds us that the human soul is created in God's image; and that image is the ideal that humanity is seeking to express, for it is the divine potential that lies at the core of our nature, and the evolutionary imperative "to be" or "to become" is the mechanism by which the unfolding of that divine potential will reach its fullest expression. Furthermore, he makes a distinction between two levels or kinds of contemplation. The first he calls "Acquired Contemplation," which he points out is acquired through our own efforts; the second he calls "Infused Contemplation," which, as the word "infused" suggests, is the result of a spiritual power taking over the soul in all of its ways. Both of his definitions share many points in common, yet there is an important distinction that separates them. He illustrates this by drawing upon the teachings of the Pseudo-Dionysius. He says:

> When the contemplation is acquired the affirm-
> ation method proceeds by adding attribute

> after attribute until the conception is formed,
> and the Negative by denying and transcending
> one attribute after another. When the con-
> templation is infused the process of affirm-
> ation is a process of discovery of His per-
> fections . . . and the process of negation one
> in which the incomparable species of God are
> infused, and the soul illuminated by a light
> by which it penetrates the unknowableness
> of His perfections.[4]

In this passage he suggests, with a subtlety typical of his order, that we might benefit by looking to the Pseudo-Dionysius for inspiration: first, to *The Divine Names* for inspiration concerning the pathway of Affirmation; and second, to *The Mystical Theology* for inspiration concerning the pathway of Negation. In *The Mystical Theology,* Dionysius explains that the affirmative method is necessary for us to grow spiritually. However, if we would know God, we must surrender ourselves to a higher will, a will that appears to the mind of the aspirant to be a vast, inaccessible mystery before which, we must inevitably, and in all humility, become absolutely still. Thus Dionysius writes:

> . . . [I]n [my earlier books] the course of
> [my] argument, as it came down from the
> highest to the lowest categories, embraced an
> ever-widening number of conceptions which
> increased at each stage of the descent, but in

---

[4] See pp. 37–38 in this publication.

[my argument now] it mounts upward from below towards the category of transcendence, and in proportion to its ascent it contracts terminology, and when the whole ascent is passed it will be totally dumb, being at last wholly united with Him Whom words cannot describe.[5]

Central to Scaramelli's thinking is the understanding that contemplation is a divine gift bestowed upon the soul rather than something that is achieved through personal effort. He makes a very interesting point concerning this when he states that the "Operation of the intellect depends on powers which are distinctly physical—the *species*[6] are transmitted by means of the external senses. . ."[7] In this he is supported to a greater or lesser degree by many of the great mystics of the Church who testify that although breaking through this limiting dependency is essential, it may be achieved only by the intervention of a spiritual influx, thus we can never earn contemplation by our own efforts. Understanding this marks the difference between those who would command the

---

[5] C. E. Rolt, trans. *Dionysius the Areopagite on The Divine Names and The Mystical Theology* (Berwick, ME: Ibis Press, 2004), p. 198.

[6] The theory of species is that each of the exterior senses is stimulated by a particular quality, which in conjunction with the exterior senses produces a sensation that is a true representation of the object concerned. For a fuller definition see pages 19–20

[7] See p. 110 in this publication.

forces of nature to take heaven by storm, and those who would walk with God. He closes the second book by posing a question about which is the most perfect life: the active life, which consists of practicing the moral virtues and the external work of charity; or the contemplative life, which consists in retirement from the world and dedicating one's life to contemplation? His answer is not so much surprising as interesting, particularly when considered in the light of his education.

In the third book, Scaramelli discusses the different grades of contemplation. The heart of human aspiration, he informs us, is expressed through prayer. In prayer we commune with the divine without pretence, standing naked, as it were, in the presence of God. There is nothing we can hide from that presence because it is the substrate of our being, thus, in prayer we commune with God and the more we commune with God the more we turn within and disentangle our soul from the vexatious preoccupation with self and become aware of God's Presence. Eventually words become meaningless and prayer becomes more of an attuning of the mind, a silent engagement with the object of our attention, which at first is driven by our desire for spiritual knowledge and experience, but is then overcome, "infused," as Scaramelli puts it, by a withdrawal of our powers into the depths of the soul wherein the person and glory of God is gradually made manifest to the soul.

Scaramelli goes on to describe the gradual spiritualization of the soul as it ascends through a series of grades toward its perfection. The first three grades he describes as a process wherein the soul grows in its awareness of the presence of God. He describes this experience as a divine invitation to contemplation, and as such it is infused. This experience is gradually intensified as the soul becomes flooded with divine light and love to the point wherein the will is united to God and the intellect illumined. In the following grades he discusses the increasingly intimate relationship between the soul and God. It is a discussion of love, of the lover, and the beloved in the way of divine union, which he describes as various grades of increasing intimacy that ultimately concludes in the Spiritual Marriage. The influence of St. Teresa d'Avila is evident throughout this chapter, particularly her great work *The Interior Castle*; and Scaramelli closes by discussing her views on the nature of the Spiritual Marriage.

The fourth book discusses the nature of certain experiences that occur during contemplation. Scaramelli lists them under three headings: visions, locutions and revelations, which he regards as being grades of contemplation. However, he warns us that they are potentially dangerous insofar as they can lead us into phantasmagoric realms of self-delusion. Both visions and locutions he divides into three classes: corporeal, imaginary, and intellectual. Corporeal visions are those that involve the exterior sense of sight, and are often unexpected manifestations. They do not indicate any sign of sanctity on the part of the recipient and should not be invested with any great significance. Imaginary visions he describes as being connected with the interior sense of fantasy (the imagination). They are interior representations of an object, produced in the imagination by means of species that are either newly combined or infused, and in either case illumined by a supernatural light which causes the object to be perceived with a clarity far greater than possible to physical sight. An intellectual vision is a one that is connected with the spiritual faculty of the intellect, and consists of a clear and certain apprehension of an object by the intellect without any form or figure being seen. Intellectual visions he divides into two classes: indistinct and distinct. The former consists of visions in which the perception of the object is absolutely clear and certain, with no doubt to its identity, yet without any perception of details. The latter includes visions in which all the details and qualities are perceived as clearly as the fact of the vision itself. The intellect, he states, is a spiritual faculty to which "God alone has access: the angels, whether good or bad, are absolutely debarred from entry therein, and illusion by means of purely intellectual vision is therefore impossible."[8]

Locutions are described as being words by which God or his saints reveal some truth to the contemplative. In a corporeal, or auricular locution, the truth is made known by God Himself, or by means of angelic intervention; voices are heard in the physical ears in just the same way as the human voice is heard. Occasionally, the locution is accompanied by a corporeal vision in which the speaker of the words

[8] See p. 130 of this publication.

is seen with the eyes. Imaginary locutions are formed in the imagination, and although nothing is heard with the bodily ears, the message is received in the mind with a clarity surpassing ordinary speech. The words are formed by means of species awakened in the imagination and illuminated with divine light, so that they are impressed on the Sensitive Appetite and received by the interior senses in a way similar to that in which the species is received by the exterior senses in normal conversation. Intellectual locutions come about in the manner employed by angels for communication, without any external voice being heard or any words in the center of the soul. The species of the concept is impressed upon the mind, which receives the concept by an act of pure understanding.

Revelations are in general an unveiling of hidden truths or a manifestation of divine secrets, by means of an infused light that imparts absolute certainty of the truth or secret revealed. The principal characteristic of a revelation is the infused light by which it is revealed. It is a light manifest in the intellect, without which no revelation can be held to occur, even though all other points should be complied with. Scaramelli closes the fourth book with a list of the various signs by which a true revelation may be known.

In the last book, Scaramelli discusses the nature of purgation and the obstacles that in some degree will inevitably beset the aspiring contemplative. He describes the path of spiritual progress as, "a process in which whatever spiritual sweetness is met with is gained only at the price of a rigorous and searching preparation,"[9] and progress is proportionate to the severity of the purgation. He discusses purgation under three headings: aridity, diabolical assaults, and troubles arising from natural causes, be they physical or moral. He defines aridity as the inability to meditate or engage in the interior work, and informs us that it is the commencement of a very dry and painful contemplation, that it is caused by the transference of the divine light from the imagination, wherein it bountifully facilitates the work of meditation, to the intellect, in which it facilitates the simple attentiveness to God. This event, however, passes unnoticed by the aspirant who, disturbed by what seems to be an inability to function effectively in meditation, is unable to perceive the subtle light that has been kindled in the intellect. He describes diabolical assault as the besieging of the soul by evil spirits for the purpose of purgation, and that such assaults; whereby an evil spirit troubles the soul, invariably consist of obsession rather than possession. Furthermore, these attacks should, if possible, be met with contempt and an absolute surrender and trust in God.

Scaramelli draws the last book to a close with a discussion about the troubles that arise from natural causes, which may take many forms, including illness; loss of friends; loss of income and position; ill-treatment and persecution from either friends or enemies. He brings to our attention that the main purpose of purgation is the purification of the soul that it might act in complete conformity with the

[9] See p. 132 of this publication.

will of God, that the Spiritual Marriage may take place in the hallowed sanctuary of a purified soul. For the Spiritual Marriage of the soul with God is a permanent relationship—the highest attainment possible in life. It is an objective which at the very least requires the dedication of one's whole life; nothing less will suffice. Furthermore, it is a path that has its dangers, and, according to Scaramelli, who echoes the opinions of many other spiritual luminaries, requires the assistance of a spiritual director well-versed in the way of experimental mystical theology.

The Handbook of Mystical Theology is not only a significant contribution to the literature of Christian spirituality but a valuable aid to any who would further their knowledge of the mystical life. It retains its importance to the present day, because Scaramelli wrote from the personal experience of a lifetime devoted to the interior life of the soul, enabling his book to transcend time and ideology. It has the added benefit of speaking in a simpler language than is usual in comparable works, making his thoughts readily accessible to the modern reader.

Scaramelli is undoubtedly one of the great instructors of the spiritual life, a shining light in the spiritual aridity of the era of the "Enlightenment" who—like Dionysius, Ruysbroeck, St. John of the Cross, and St. Teresa before him—guides the aspiring soul with the surety of one who has truly known the Divine Union, and consequently knows of what he speaks. His work was a seed that slowly grew until it finally flowered 150 years after his death in a movement that arose within Catholic Christianity at the dawn of the twentieth century, a movement that made accessible to souls hungry for the spiritual life a rich legacy whereby Divine Union and the Spiritual Marriage could be attained. Not all of the great names concerned—Butler, Poulain, von Hugel, Evelyn Underhill, Waite and others—acknowledged their debt to Scaramelli, but they all built upon foundations that he had laid. It is well for us to remember that what we owe to them, we owe also to him.

Allan Armstrong
Prior of the
Order of Dionysis & Paul
August 2005

PREFACE

THE vital element in Mysticism does not fall within the category of subjects which can be taught by books or communicated in the rites of any mystery in their entirety, for it is essentially an experience which must be undergone by each individual in his own person, and made his own by each. Mysticism as a whole comprises, in effect, a series of attempts made at all periods of man's history along two distinct yet interdependent lines. It aims, in the first place, at grasping the truth that lies behind all form, at getting into touch with the spirit which is concealed behind the letter of the word, and at penetrating the veil of appearance to the reality behind, and in such endeavour lies the

5

experience which is of its essence.   In
the second place, and in direct dependence on the experience, is the attempt
to communicate to those who have
not seen it something of the splendour
of the Divine Light.   There can be no
question but that the words of those
who report will be halting and finally
insufficient, for we have no language
for the things of God ; but there is no
serious doubt of their being also
sufficient for the purpose of witness-
ing to the great facts of the spiritual
life, and of offering some encourage-
ment to those who aspire to its glories
and its pains.   The ultimate experience, it is evident, can never be
obtained vicariously, but before it is
reached there are many degrees of
preparation wherein the adventures
of forerunners in the same path may
bring both comfort and warning.

Mysticism is obviously not the pre-
rogative of any one church or of any
one school of thought—it is rather the
search for the life which stands behind

and is manifesting through all such institutions—for there is no monopoly in the things of the spirit. But just as there are in the religion of the East certain characteristics which distinguish it from that of the West, so it has become possible to draw a broad distinction between the theories and the methods of eastern and western mysticism. With those of the East we are not now concerned; those of the West have unquestionably been reduced to whatever degree of order is possible by the Roman Catholic Church more effectively than by any other body. The purpose of the present abridgment is to give as concisely as possible the main positions held by that Church with regard to certain large questions of the mystical life, as they are expounded by one of its authoritative writers. No comment, favourable or otherwise, has been made on those positions, for it is not that works on the subject are felt to be lacking, but to be generally so comprehensive as to be beyond the resources, both as to time and money, of a large number of people to whom the subject is one of vivid interest.

It may very well be questioned whether classification and analysis of so elusive matters as mystical states are possible in any effective sense, and whether, if they be possible, they are desirable. There is no doubt that in Mystical Theology, as in other fields of enquiry, the business of the enquirer is chiefly that of deducing general rules from a large number of particular instances; but, even more than the ordinary scientist, the enquirer who takes the life of the spirit for his province is bound to avoid regarding those general rules as anything but the roughest approximations to the facts of any particular case. The most accurate and detailed analysis of mystical states can never do more than offer, in any individual case, points in aid of diagnosis—the real judgment of a spiritual condition will probably depend just as much on intuition as in the case of physical medicine. And yet anything which can aid to just that extent of providing points of departure for the real diagnosis is of unquestionable value in so stupendous yet delicate a matter as that of spiritual health and progress, for here the question of right treatment is at least equally important as in the case of physical health. A comprehension of the ways of the spirit, that is, is important not only for curing the diseases of the spirit, but also for keeping it in balance and health, and an accurate classification of spiritual states may also serve to decide (where such a thing is in question) what degree of mystical progress has been arrived at in any actual case.

Il Direttorio Mistico, of which the following pages are an abridgment, is the work of a Jesuit Father who was born at Rome in 1687 and died at Macerata in 1752. He entered the Society of Jesus at the age of nineteen,

and spent some thirty years in active
ministry as a missionary. He was the
author of five works in all, of which
the most important are the two
Directories, *Il Direttorio Ascetico* and *Il
Direttorio Mistico*. The former, which
consists of a treatise on the ordinary
means to Christian perfection as
distinguished from the extraordinary
means of contemplation, was translated into English in 1870-1 and
published at Dublin in four volumes.
The latter appeared originally at
Venice in 1754, two years after its
author's death, and subsequently went
through several editions, and was
translated into Latin, French, German,
Spanish, and Polish, but, it seems,
never into English. The latest edition
in the original Italian appeared in 1900.
In its original form it deals with all
points and stages of the contemplative
life with a great wealth of argument
and example, and also with several
controversial questions, such as
Quietism, of which no mention has

been made in the abridgment, as being beyond its scope.

One thing should be noticed with regard to the method of classification that Scaramelli employed. In addition to the principal states and stages of the interior life, he included as states certain conditions which were really modes of states rather than separate states in themselves. Father Poulain has pointed this out in several places in his criticisms of Scaramelli's classification,[1] and in some cases Scaramelli was apparently conscious of the fact himself. He has, for example, treated of the Divine Touches as if they were a separate state,

---

[1] See *The Graces of Interior Prayer*, by R. P. Poulain, S.J., ch. 6. 15, ch. 9. 26, ch. 18. 51, and the Bibliographical Index, No. 110, where he speaks of the classification as giving " as distinct *degrees*, having a fixed place in the mystic ladder, conditions which are simply manners of being of the prayer of quiet, as well as of ecstasy (silence, inebriation, the anguish of love, touches, etc.). It is true, however, that these graces are received in a *higher measure* in the more exalted unions." See also ch. 30. 9.

making part of the chain leading to the Spiritual Marriage, and yet he expressly says that they belong to the state of union and are part of the experience of that state. But it is not, as a matter of fact, difficult, on a little consideration, to distinguish the states which are well defined from those which are in reality more properly regarded as ways of being of different states. Of the eleven which Scaramelli describes, the grades of Spiritual Silence, the Intoxication of Love, Spiritual Sleep, the Thirst of Love and Divine Touches, as well, I think, as Ecstasy and Rapture, may be regarded as merging into the Prayer of Recollection, the Prayer of Quiet, the Simple Union and the perfect and lasting Union which is the Spiritual Marriage, as different modes of those states. These four, together with the Purgations, remain as definite stages on the path of the reintegration of the Spirit of man in the Spirit which is God.   D. H. S. NICHOLSON.

A HANDBOOK OF
MYSTICAL THEOLOGY

I

PRELIMINARY

FOR the proper comprehension of Mystical Theology as a whole, it is necessary to distinguish between that which is experimental and that which is doctrinal. Experimental Mystical Theology is a pure knowledge of God which the soul receives in the bright darkness of some high contemplation, together with so intimate an experience of love that it is utterly lost to itself and united and transformed in God. It thus embraces the actual experiences of the mystic. Doctrinal Mystical Theology is, on the other

Mystical Theology, Experimental and Doctrinal.

15

hand, a science, the business of which is to examine the above experiences, and to draw from them what conclusions it may with regard to their essential qualities and effects. It has further to frame rules for the safe conduct of those who are already in a state of contemplation, and for the help of those who have not yet arrived at such a state. As a science, then, it is both speculative and practical, and on its practical side is employed by the Spiritual Directors without whom not even the most holy contemplative can progress safely on his way. The possession of a Director versed in Experimental Mystical Theology is absolutely indispensable at all stages of contemplation, for in the first place mystical experience alone does not suffice for spiritual good conduct or for the best use of the gifts of contemplation, and in the second the contemplative is so open to illusion and self-deception that some external authority is necessary.

But inasmuch as contemplation is a
free gift of God, it must not be thought
that Doctrinal Mystical Theology pro-
poses any definite instruction which
will inevitably result in contemplation.
Its office is solely that of preparation
for the reception of such a gift, and
the direction of those who have already
received it : as to its ultimate acquisition, the soul must remain indifferent
in the hands of God, and be content
to receive just so much as may be
given.

To understand the manner in which Psycho-
action takes place (including the logical basis.
actions occurring in the contemplative
state) it is necessary to give a short
account of the theory of psychology
which is contained in the writings of
St Thomas Aquinas and the scholastics generally, and has been steadfastly adhered to by the Church.

Man is composed of two parts, viz.,
the rational mind, under which are
grouped intellect, memory, and will,
with which he performs spiritual

2

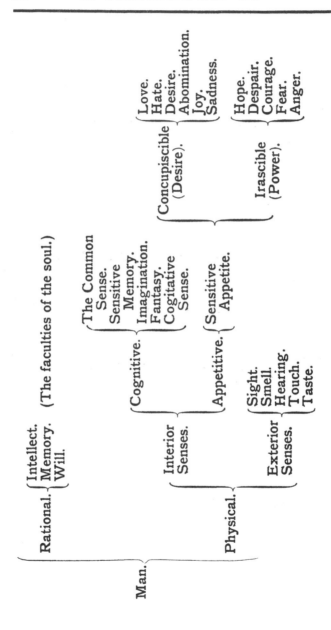

Man.

Rational. { Intellect. Memory. Will. (The faculties of the soul.)

Physical.

Interior Senses.

Cognitive. { The Common Sense. Sensitive Memory. Imagination. Fantasy. Cogitative Sense.

Appetitive. { Sensitive Appetite.

Concupiscible (Desire). { Love. Hate. Desire. Abomination. Joy. Sadness.

Irascible (Power). { Hope. Despair. Courage. Fear. Anger.

Exterior Senses. { Sight. Smell. Hearing. Touch. Taste.

actions, and the physical part, to which are attributed exterior and interior senses, by means of which material actions are performed.

The interior senses attributed to the physical part are treated of first, and these in their turn are divided into Cognitive and Appetitive (or conative). The cognitive senses are the common sense, imagination, fantasy, the cogitative sense, and the sensitive memory; though whether in effect these are separate faculties or only one faculty is not of importance for the present subject. The common sense is conceived as a power situated in the brain, to which all the exterior senses transmit their *species* of any object, and by means of these *species* the common sense forms the idea of the object. The theory of *species* is that each of the exterior senses is put into motion by a *species impressa*, a quality, that is, which in conjunction with the exterior sense produces a sensation. The sensation produced

The Physical Part.

is a true representation of the object contracted by the exterior sense, and it is this sensation which is transmitted to the common sense and is called the *species expressa*, since it expresses the object in question.[1] The common sense, then, is the power of the cognitive senses which receives the *species expressæ*, and by their means forms the idea. That function of the cognitive senses which has the power of preserving the *species* received is called the sensitive memory; that function of them which, depending on the memory, forms images like the original *species*, is called the imagina-

[1] For a discussion on the theory of the *species*, see *Psychology*, by M. Maher, S.J., 1905, pp. 51-4. "The *species* is not an entity which has immigrated into the mind from the object, but a modification or disposition awakened in the mind by the action of the object." "The *species* is not an intermediate representation *from which* the mind infers the object, but a psychical modification *by which* the mind is likened, or conformed, to the object and thus determined to cognize it." The book contains a full statement of the mediæval position with regard to psychology.

tion; the function which combines together the *species* of things which are not present is called the fantasy, and the function which judges roughly of the desirability or undesirability of anything is called the cogitative sense.

To the cognitive senses, and as part therefore of the interior senses, is linked the sensitive appetite. This is a faculty which depends on the cognitive senses, and is a power of desire the object of which is the sensible good or the sensible evil (as a thing to be escaped from) which is represented to it by the imagination or fantasy. In itself it is blind, and moves blindly to or from the good or evil things which are represented to it; in itself it has no initiative whatever. It is this which constitutes the lower part in man, as distinguished from the higher part of which the motive force is reason and the light of faith. To the sensitive appetite are attributed two faculties by means of which it acts

—the concupiscible, which is concerned with sensible good or evil as things to be sought or avoided, and the irascible, which is occupied with the difficulties to be overcome in that proceeding. These two faculties, therefore, are very closely connected ; the irascible faculty is the auxiliary which provides the force by which the concupiscible faculty moves and works. The actions of the sensitive appetite are the eleven chief passions : Love, Hate, Desire, Abomination (the desire of avoidance), Joy, Sadness, Hope, Despair, Courage, Fear, and Anger. Of these, Love, Hate, Desire, Abomination, Joy, and Sadness are referable to the concupiscible faculty of the sensitive appetite, inasmuch as they cause a movement either to or from an object ; Hope, Despair, Courage, Fear, and Anger are referred to the irascible faculty because they provide the force for such movement.

The Rational Part.   The specific characteristic of man is, however, the rational part (comprising the intellect, the memory, and the will), which is the source of spiritual actions. For cognition by the intellect to be possible, it is necessary for it to receive the *species* as in the case of the interior senses, but, inasmuch as the intellect is pure spirit, it cannot receive the *species* of so gross a thing as a material object. The aid of the images of the imagination is therefore called in, and these images, illuminated by the light of the intellect, enable the *species* to be received. The *species intelligibilis* thus produced is sufficient for spiritual cognition—the images themselves not being in their original gross condition, but purged from materiality by the light of the intellect. The office of the memory is the preservation of these *species* after the immediate cognition has passed. The will is an appetitive (conative) power which has as its object good and evil, and is in itself blind but free. Of itself it has no initiative, but (similarly to the sensitive appetite) is put into motion by the cognitions which are received from the object. It is thus impossible for the will to be said to love without any cognition of its object—*nihil volitum quin præcognitum*—although in certain grades of contemplation the cognition is so spiritual and subtle that it is scarcely discernible by the intellect. The point in which the will differs from the sensitive appetite is that the actions of the latter occur in conjunction with some physical change, which may even be noticed externally, as a sudden change of colour, whereas in the case of the will no such physical change occurs, but there is simply a movement of the rational power.[1] The will properly has command over all the inferior powers, but since the fall of man the imagination and the sensitive appetite have shaken off its yoke, and are rebels against its authority.

[1] Cf. *Psychology*, M. Maher, S. J., p. 209. "Of conscious appetite the schoolmen recognised two kinds as essentially distinct—rational and sensitive. The former has its source in intellectual, the latter in sensuous, apprehension."

The whole procedure may be summed up in an example. The eye falls on an object, which transmits to it the *species*, by means of which the eye forms its vision. The *species* is in turn transmitted to the common sense, and that forthwith produces the image which puts the sensitive appetite in motion either to or from the object, according as it appears desirable or the reverse. The image, in conjunction with the intellect, produces the *species intelligibilis*, and from this results the cognition, the *species* of which is preserved in the memory. Lastly, the will, according to the desirability or otherwise of the cognition, agrees with or resists the impulse of the appetite.

All the above, however, is quite in- sufficient to produce even the lowest act of supernatural contemplation, for such acts are far above our natural powers, and belong properly to the order of grace. The graces necessary for the purpose are two : (1) Sanctifying grace, by which man is given a new divine being, and raised to the sonship of God. Consequently upon the action of this grace man receives the infused habits of the theological virtues, which enable him to perform acts of faith, hope, and charity. The distinction between an infused and an acquired habit is that the latter is produced by resistance and effort; the former produces an inclination to the virtues. For putting this inclination into action a further grace is necessary, viz. : (2) Actual grace, which consists in a supernatural illumination of the intellect by God, and certain interior emotions by which He puts the will into motion. It is prevenient inasmuch as it arouses man to the good, and works in him without his consent; concomitant inasmuch as it goes with him and impels him to consent to the good (this, therefore, includes man's own consent); and subsequent inasmuch as it follows him so that he may bring the work to perfection. For any meritorious and supernatural act, then, this actual grace is necessary, arousing as it does the sanctifying grace to action; and conversely all acts dependent on these two graces are supernatural. The application of this to acts of contemplation is that they are supernatural because they consist in acts of faith and charity, and these virtues proceed from the infused habits which are received with the sanctifying grace, and put into motion by the actual grace.

One thing further is necessary for contemplation, and that is the influx of the gifts of the Holy Spirit. The seven gifts are: Wisdom, Understanding, Knowledge, and Counsel, belonging to the intellect; and Strength, Piety, and the Fear of God, which are referred to the will. In so far as they are habitual they are received with the sanctifying grace, and produce an inclination towards obedience to the impulses of the spirit; but

The Gifts of the Holy Spirit.

for contemplation to be possible they must be actual—they must actually move the soul to the extraordinary and superhuman actions in which contemplation consists.

II

CONTEMPLATION
GENERALLY

IT is not to be supposed that contem- Contempla- tion and plation, however great its value, is a Medita- tion. necessary means to perfection. The ordinary means thereto is meditation, which is the mother of contemplation in the sense that it prepares the way with its laborious use of the mind; while contemplation is the extra-ordinary means. Both methods produce the same benefits, but they are acquired by meditation more slowly and with more fatigue than by contemplation: "meditation seeks God by means of discursive thought, contemplation possesses Him." It is the greatest possible mistake to attempt to contemplate—deliberately to suspend, that is, the use of the mind—

before the time is ripe, or to cling to meditation when there is a definite call to contemplation. The signs by which this call may be known are given by St John of the Cross,[1] and are as follows :

The signs of readiness for Contemplation.   1. Inability to meditate any more. The use of the interior faculties for imagination and discursive thought is felt to be checked, and there is great difficulty and aridity in thinking about the subject of meditation. This in itself, however, is not enough, as it may be caused by lack of energy or carelessness.

2. In spite of this inability to meditate on the things of heaven, there is no desire to turn to the things of the world. If this desire exist, the inability to meditate is not a sign of readiness for contemplation. But this again is not a certain test, as it may have some merely physical cause. The supreme criterion is :

3. There must be during prayer a

[1] *Ascent of Mount Carmel*, Bk. 2, ch. 13-14.

certain loving looking to God. It consists in a turning of the attention to Him with a feeling of love and great interior peace, and is really the beginning of contemplation, caused by an illumination which is sometimes so pure that there is no consciousness of it, but only the realisation of its effect in the sensation of peace, and an inclination to virtue.

Nevertheless, it does not follow that, because a person has been raised to contemplation, he should give up the practice of meditation entirely. If, on any occasion of prayer, the contemplative state is not reached, he must return to meditation without delay or hesitation.

Mystical contemplation may be defined as an elevation of the mind in God, or in things which are divine, with a simple look of admiration and love of those things. N.B. It is precisely in this "simple look" that contemplation differs from meditation, for in the latter its place is taken by re-

Definition of Contemplation, and its difference from Meditation.

peated acts of the intellect and the imagination, searching for the truth by means of their activities, whereas in contemplation these activities are rendered unnecessary by the simple look with which the truth is discerned. The two cases are comparable to the condition of the audience in a theatre before and after the raising of the curtain; before it is raised they guess and speculate about the arrangement of the stage—and this is similar to the process of meditation; but when the curtain is up they see, without further need of imagination—and this is the manner of contemplation. The magnitude of the truth and the clearness with which it is seen, render it inevitable that the feeling of admiration should be present; and so necessary is this that one authority holds that without such admiration the contemplative state has not been reached.[1] That the look should be also a look of love is necessary to distinguish contempla-

[1] Alvarez de Paz, vol. iii., book 5, pt. 2, ch. 1.

tion from the sight of the truth gained by the philosophers.

With regard to the attainment of contemplation it must be particularly remembered

1. That contemplation must be preceded by meditation, except in very rare cases.

2. That no deliberate attempt should be made to reach the contemplative state, either by emptying the mind of all thoughts and ideas, or by fixing the mind or any object without discursive thought. Contemplation is the free gift of God.

3. That there is therefore no set period at the end of which meditation will pass into contemplation.

Contemplation is divided into (1) Acquired (or active or natural) and (2) Infused (or passive or supernatural).

1. Acquired contemplation is that which may follow from our own efforts with the help of grace, and especially with long practice in meditation, although strictly speaking contem-

Acquired Contemplation.

3

plation is not due to those efforts. The truth is that this contemplation is arrived at very often after a great effort has been made to adhere to the virtues, and to meditate deeply, and it therefore *appears* to be the result of those efforts. As a matter of fact, although it is proportioned to the progress made in meditation, it is essentially a free gift.

Infused Contempla-tion.   2. Infused contemplation is that which, although some disposition towards it is presupposed, does not depend in any way on the efforts which have been made, but solely on the will of God.

The two kinds of contemplation have therefore certain points in common, viz. :

1. They are both a simple look of admiration and love to divine things, although the sight of those things may be greater or in some way different in infused contemplation.

2. In both of them a certain disposition is presupposed, although in

infused contemplation this predisposition—in respect of purification and virtue—is the greater.

The differences between them are more numerous, viz. : Points of difference between the two.

1. Acquired contemplation depends to some extent on our own efforts, with the help of grace; infused contemplation depends on grace alone.

2. Acquired contemplation is arrived at little by little—step by step until the light shines out from God; infused contemplation occurs suddenly and unexpectedly.

3. Acquired contemplation never occurs out of prayer, on which it depends; infused contemplation often occurs out of prayer.

4. Acquired contemplation is never concerned with matters other than those already in the mind; infused contemplation often has as its object some entirely different and unexpected truth.

5. The feelings of admiration and love which are felt are much stronger

in infused than in acquired contemplation.

6. The higher grades of union (*e.g.* Ecstasy or Rapture) are never the result of acquired contemplation.

7. In acquired contemplation it is always possible to turn away from the object of it; in infused contemplation it is impossible of one's own will to detach oneself from the object or to reflect on one's own acts.

8. Infused contemplation is much less subject than acquired contemplation to disturbances arising from the fantasy.

Contemplation by Affirmation and Negation.   Both acquired and infused contemplation of God may occur in either of two ways, by affirmation, that is, and by negation. Contemplation by way of affirmation is contemplation in which perfections conceivable by humanity, such as justness, wisdom, etc., are attributed to God, and a pure and simple conception of Him is formed, in which there is no tinge of imperfection. Contemplation by way of negation is the result of the position that the human intellect has no other *species* than such as are derived from the senses, and therefore none by which the divine perfection can be expressed. Such perfections as humanity can conceive are therefore denied to God, and similar perfections of a sublimity above our conception are attributed to Him, with the result that an abstract but positive and exalted conception is formed, which inclines towards indistinctness and confusion. The former is similar to the method of a painter producing a picture by laying on colour after colour, the latter to that of a sculptor producing a statue by chipping from the block of marble all that is unfitting for his result; and of the two methods the latter is preferable, and the one generally employed in the higher grades of infused contemplation. When the contemplation is acquired the affirmative method proceeds by adding attribute after attribute until the conception is formed, and the negative by denying and transcending one attribute after another. When the contemplation is infused the process of affirmation is a process of discovery of His perfections to the contemplative by God, and the process of negation one in which the incomparable *species* of God are infused, and the soul illuminated by a light by which it penetrates the unknowableness of His perfections. This is the Vision in Darkness, by which the soul is united to God in an ignorance of all things.[1]

The Cooperation of the Fantasy in Contemplation. The question of the co-operation of the fantasy in acts of contemplation is one which has been the cause of considerable disagreement among theologians, but the true answer as to whether the fantasy does so co-operate or not is to be found by making a distinction between the lower and higher grades of contemplation. It has been already shown[2] that the

[1] See further, p. 113.   [2] See p. 25.

operation of the intellect depends on powers which are distinctly physical— the *species* are either transmitted by means of the external senses, or, if the intellect takes the initiative, the fantasy follows in its wake. In either case there is an interaction between the two faculties, and it is because of this natural interaction that the fantasy is conceived to co-operate in the lower grades of contemplation. It has to be remembered, however, that in such contemplations the intellect does not limit itself to the actual *species* before it—it uses them rather as points of departure for higher thoughts concerning God. To break down this interaction a greater force is necessary than is to be found in the lower grades, and this takes the form either of a *species intelligibilis* which is infused into the intellect, and is intrinsically supernatural, or an illumination which elevates to a higher level the *species intelligibilis* that has been acquired, and so renders the fantasy inoperative.

Purely
Intellectual
Contempla-
tion.

Thus in the higher grades the contemplation is purely intellectual, without any of that co-operation of the fantasy inevitable in the lower grades. The word "co-operation" is to be understood in the sense that although the fantasy may precede the intellectual contemplation, as in the case of the *species intelligibilis* that has been acquired, or may follow it with an attempt to reproduce what is thereby comprehended, it does not co-operate effectively in its production. If the contemplation is purely intellectual the attempt to reproduce the experience is necessarily inadequate : it is in the cases where the fantasy has effectively co-operated in producing the contemplation that the power of reproduction is in any way commensurate with the experience. For this reason those contemplations wherein the intellectual vision of the truth is the principal one, and the part of the fantasy is only secondary, are preferable to purely intellectual visions on the one hand, and those which are merely the work of the fantasy on the other.

Purely intellectual contemplation, as defined above, is met with, then, only in the higher grades.[1] It occurs without question in the Union of Love, in the state known as Spiritual Sleep, in Intellectual Visions and certain Locutions.[2]

There are certain essential qualities of contemplation, as distinct from its effects, which are always found in the contemplative state while it is in actual progress. They are best grouped under three heads, viz.:

Essential Qualities of Contemplation.

1. Suspension of the mind in God. This is more than the elevation of the mind referred to in the definition of contemplation, inasmuch as it supposes a greater penetration into the divine things, and a more profound tranquillity therein. It is in fact a

[1] For the classification and analysis of the grades, see Part III.

[2] See Part IV.

perfect attention to the divine object of contemplation, accompanied by complete forgetfulness of everything else, and it is the perfection of this attention which distinguishes contemplation from meditation, for in the latter case thoughts extraneous to the object of meditation are common.

2. An indescribable delight and joy, which may be confined to the higher part of the soul, or may overflow to the lower part and fill the interior senses with delight. In certain cases this sweetness reaches as far as the exterior senses, which receive it under the form of perfumes and tastes and music.

3. An interior peace felt in all the parts of the personality.

Effects of Contemplation. The effects of contemplation, which are distinguished from its essential qualities by remaining in the soul when the contemplative state is over, will be dealt with in detail in considering the different grades. They are included under the heads of humility, detachment from earthly things, freedom from shortcomings, a desire for physical mortification, strength in suffering, abnegation of one's own will and judgment, and love of one's neighbour in every form.

Remembering always that man can never earn contemplation by his own efforts, it is yet true that there are certain predispositions which facilitate its acquisition. These are more particularly a sincere attempt to attain to solitude, by which is not meant fleeing from society, but doing what has to be done without being immersed in it, and so leaving the mind free to commune with God; detachment from earthly things; purity of heart; extirpation of passions and vices, and therefore mortification to the point of not resenting ill-usage, of feeling no overpowering pleasure or regret in the gain or loss of property, and of not being subject to importunate thoughts during prayer; and contempt of the honour of the world. In

Predispositions to Contemplation.

a word, the perfection of the active life is the proper preparation for the contemplative life. The last predisposition is continual prayer, both vocal and mental, and the practice of the presence of God.

Which is the most Perfect Life? Which, then, is the most perfect life, the active (which consists in practising the moral virtues and the external works of charity), the contemplative (which consists in retirement from all external works, and consecration to the work of contemplation), or the mixed, which partakes of both the above, passing from contemplation to the external works of charity, and *vice versa*?

The first is admittedly good, the second is better, but the last, the mixed life, is the best of all, for it has the perfections of both the others. "To burn in contemplation, and to communicate to others the light of one's inward fire—this is perfection."

III

THE GRADES OF CONTEMPLATION

ALTHOUGH the grades of con-templation are in reality infinite, it is customary to classify them under certain headings for their better comprehension. The main division is between those which are indistinct, wherein the divine object is represented with a certain luminous obscurity, and of these the consummation is mystical union with God, and those which are distinct, wherein the object and the truth are seen clearly, as in the case of visions, locutions, and revelations. It has to be remembered that the grades of the former class are not to be conceived as inevitably following in the order in which they

45

are given, because inasmuch as contemplation is a gift of God there can
be no absolute rule : all that can be
done is to give the order in which the
grades are found to occur in the
vast majority of cases. The grades of
distinct contemplation, on the other
hand, have no precise order amongst
themselves, nor can they be said to
occur at any particular point of the
procession of grades of indistinct
contemplation. It is for this reason
that they are treated of separately,
in Part IV.

Prayer of Infused Re-collection. The first grade is the Prayer of Recollection—infused recollection, that
is, for acquired recollection is not
properly a grade of contemplation,
inasmuch as it is the result of human
effort. Infused recollection is a sudden
calm retreat of all the interior powers
into the depths of the soul, wherein
God manifests Himself to them. It
is brought about by the flooding
of the intellect and the will with

light and sweetness, which overflow, so to speak, into the interior
senses and hold them united before
God in the inmost places of the soul
where He is manifested. It is the
answer of all the parts of the personality of man to the call of God within,
so that they are concentrated on the
splendour of the indwelling Deity:
it is the result of the sudden intimate
conviction that God really is within.
The effect of this vivid conviction is
so great that the exterior senses are
affected as well; the eyes close naturally, nothing is heard, and the body
is disinclined to move. Infused recollection comes as a rule quite suddenly
and unexpectedly, even when there is
no thought of God; and it must be
remembered that it is more in the
nature of a beginning—a call to contemplation on the part of God—than
a grade of perfect contemplation itself. Meditation, for example, and
the working of the intellect should
not be discarded, for the faculties of

the soul[1] are not suspended, but rather concentrated on God, and must therefore continue to act, though very peacefully. A too great energy of action would only result in dissipating the influence and disturbing the interior peace: to persist in vocal prayer, for example, when this sudden concentration on the indwelling God is felt, would be mistaken zeal. God is within, and the realisation of this is the first step in contemplation: the recipients of the Prayer of infused Recollection should therefore seek Him within themselves in prayer.

Its Effects. The effects of this first grade are a greater detachment from the things of the world, since the soul has had some experience of the sweetness of the things of God, and a correspondingly greater love of prayer and solitude than was felt before, since these are realised to be the means of a renewal of that experience.

[1] The faculties of the soul are the intellect, the memory, and the will. See pp. 18 and 23.

The grade of Spiritual Silence is Spiritual Silence. distinct from that of Recollection on the one hand, and the Prayer of Quiet on the other. It is in reality an intensification of the Prayer of Recollection, and is defined as a suspension in which the faculties of the soul are not lost, but simply astonished before God. The light and the love which flooded the faculties in the preceding grade are intensified herein, but they are not yet strong enough to prevent the intellect and the will detaching themselves when they like from the object of contemplation. While the state lasts the imagination and the fantasy do not interrupt with extraneous thoughts, the intellect and the will are silent with amazement, and the sensitive appetite reflects the peace of those higher faculties. It is like the absolute stillness of all the parts of the personality which is experienced at some sudden and stupendous view : a moderate emotion demands expression, but such an overpower-

4

ing experience as this is only adequately expressed by silence. And it may be that in this silence and great stillness God speaks to the listening soul. It is undesirable, therefore, in this state that any attempt should be made to use the intellect, for that would only have the effect of breaking the silence, but when the state has passed return should be made to all the activities of prayer. The duration of the state, without any break, is short—in one stretch it seldom continues for as long as half an hour.

Its Duration.

Its Effects.   The effects of Spiritual Silence are similar to those of the Prayer of Recollection, though intensified.

The Prayer of Quiet.   The Prayer of Quiet is a rest and internal sweetness arising in the depths of the soul, occasionally overflowing into the physical faculties and senses, and caused by the closeness of the soul to God and the feeling of His presence. It is distinguished from Spiritual Silence by the fact that that state is the result especially of an illumination of the intellect, while the Prayer of Quiet arises from an experimental love (of the will) which actually feels the presence of God. This sensation of God present is the essence of the Prayer of Quiet, and its immediate effect is a very deep interior peace welling up from the depths of the soul and spreading gradually throughout all the personality. The best simile is perhaps that suggested by Saint Teresa, where she likens the spreading of this peace to the fumes of a censer penetrating from the centre to all parts and recesses of the soul; and the intensity of the feeling is so great that it seems impossible to conceive a higher delight or a more profound peace. In some cases the sensation is confined to the faculties of the soul, and in others it spreads to the physical faculties and senses, but the Prayer of Quiet may perfectly well be present without any physical sensation at all. Its essence is the feeling of the presence of God.

In this grade the will is united to God, but the union is imperfect—it is united to the presence of God, but not to His substance, and it is not transformed in Him. From this imperfection of the union it results that the will is still capable of certain peaceful acts of gratitude and humiliation; in the case of perfect union no acts at all are possible. The intellect, the imagination, and the memory are as a rule neither united nor suspended, but free to act, and can reflect on what is happening within the soul. It is also possible for them to be concerned with extraneous objects, so long as they are not definitely evil, but this causes great difficulty and disturbance to the peace of the soul. The advice is, therefore, that no attention should be paid to them, but that they should be left to their own devices, while the will remains intent on the object of contemplation.

The duration of the Prayer of Quiet Its Dura-
is said by Saint Teresa to be some- tion.
times as much as several days, during
which time (in the later stages of the
grade) the intellect and imagination
and other faculties can not only be
concerned with exterior works in the
service of God, but are actually helped
in the execution of those services.
The will is fixed throughout on the
end, which is God, while the other
faculties are occupied with His service, which is a means to that end; a
suggestive parallel is that of medicine
being taken as a means to the end of
health, where the will is fixed on the
end, while the mind is concerned with
the means. Saint Teresa adds, however, that while the state is in progress the faculties are incapable of
attending to anything which is not
the service of God—for entirely mun-
dane affairs there is no capacity whatever to act.

The effects of this state are more Its Effects.
particularly :

1. A feeling of great humility and comparative worthlessness before so great a splendour.

2. A disinterested love of God, which has for motive neither hope of reward nor fear of punishment.

3. An immense trust in God, and some certainty of salvation.

In common with all other grades of contemplation, the Prayer of Quiet must not be sought by means of human effort, but when it is received discursive thoughts should be abandoned so long as it continues, because the purpose of discursive thought is precisely that of arousing the will, and in this case the will is already aroused by the divine action. The attitude should rather be one of absolute abandonment in the hands of God, standing before Him, as it were, in complete peace and readiness to do His will. It should be remembered that the soul has not yet reached by any means the state of Perfect Union, and therefore is still far from its full degree of strength, and should accordingly be sheltered from occupations likely to distract it from its term. Many travel as far as this point, but few go further, and it is here that the danger of falling back is greatest.

The grade known as the Intoxication of Love is of two kinds—imperfect and perfect. Intoxication of Love.

That which is imperfect is conceded to beginners who have passed through neither of the purgations,[1] and is an unimaginably sweet love kindled in the sensitive appetite, and manifested externally in sudden movements of the body, and extraordinary and uncontrollable actions. It has all the marks of physical drunkenness—the desire to shout and cry and dance and sing—and is, in a word, a furious exultation of joy. Although it has its source in the rational faculties, it is kindled in the senses, and from the sensitive appetite extends to the ex- Imperfect.

[1] See Part V.

terior senses. For this reason it is far from perfect, although it is the highest gift that can be received by a soul which has not undergone purgation.

Its Effects. Its effects are an even greater detachment from the world and attachment to God, with a corresponding energy in mortification and self-annihilation.

A certain moderation in these transports is desirable, because their excess may easily cause physical disturbances, such as palpitation of the heart, which in their turn may result in inability to pray. An attempt should be made to restrain the force from manifesting externally, by an attempt to receive the communication more entirely with the intellect, and, if necessary, by directing the mind on some other object or by cutting short the time of prayer.

Perfect. The perfect Intoxication of Love is only dealt with here for convenience; it is in reality a very high state which is only conceded to those who have been nearly or entirely purified by purgation. It is a communication in the spiritual part, of great joy, and if it overflows into the physical faculties and senses it is only because of its great fulness, and not because the physical effects are in any way of its essence. It is a high contemplation, in reality a very exalted form of the Prayer of Quiet, which causes so splendid and joyful a love in the soul that it dies to all earthly things, and breaks out into the ravings of a glorious madness. The eccentricities and disconnectedness are more in the interior actions than in the exterior, as is the case with imperfect intoxication, and Saint Teresa describes the state as one in which the soul is so overflowing with joy that it simply does not know what it is doing, or whether it should talk or be silent, or laugh or cry. The faculties of the soul are neither bound nor free : not the former, for the state is not yet

that of Union (wherein the faculties
are wholly bound) although it is very
near it, and not the latter, for the
faculties have the capacity of concerning themselves with things other
than God, though they do not do

**Its Dura-
tion.** so. The state may last one or more
days, though during this time it
will not be at the same level of
vividness.

Its Effects. Besides the effects of detachment,
etc., common to the grades already
described, and intensified in the
present grade, there is also an impulse
to break out into shouts of tremendous
praise of God, and a very fervent
desire to suffer for Him. There is an
almost incredible strength to work
for the divine ends, and very often an
unexpected ability to give a metrical
expression to the emotions.

**The Spark
of Love.** What is known as the Spark of
Love is regarded as a less perfect
example of perfect Intoxication, its
effects being almost exactly the same,
though its duration is less.

There are also two varieties of Spiritual Sleep, of which the first is the result of the perfect Intoxication just described. It consists in a very fervent love, in which the will lets all cognition go, and abandons itself to sleep in the arms of the Beloved. The exterior senses and the very soul are also asleep, the only faculty that remains slightly conscious being the intellect, and this only to the extent necessary to provide the degree of cognition without which love is impossible. The faculties are in effect not fully suspended, but there is no consciousness of the manner of their operation. It is perhaps best expressed by the words of the Song of Solomon, "I sleep, but my heart waketh." The effects are similar to those of perfect Intoxication.

The second variety is produced by a flooding of the soul with light, which results in a complete oblivion wherein there is no capacity to reflect on any acts which are performed, and after which there is no kind of memory of what has occurred. The characteristics of the state are that the fantasy and the memory are inoperative, and the relation with God is so delicate that it is not perceived by the intellect or the will. Without these characteristics it is evident that some memory of the state would remain after its conclusion, whereas in effect several hours may pass in a flash, and leave no idea either of themselves or of their occupation.

Its Effects. The occurrence of the state can, therefore, only be recognised by the effects which follow it, and these are in particular a recollection and elevation of the mind to God, accompanied by a great measure of detachment from the world and from all forms and imaginary figures, and the feeling of a great peace within. The chief point of difference between the two varieties of Spiritual Sleep is that there is a glimmer of consciousness left in the first, which is strictly more comparable to sleepiness than actual sleep, and no consciousness whatever in the second; and it is this complete oblivion which distinguishes it also from Ecstasy, where the senses are equally lost, but the ability to notice and remember are retained.

The second kind of Spiritual Sleep is very close to the Mystical Union of Love, and so not generally conceded till considerable progress has been made in contemplation.

The Thirst of Love is the name given to that passionate desire for God which is the result of some experience of Him and a great love for Him, but when He is not yet possessed, in the sense of the Spiritual Marriage. The name is applied especially to this desire when it is experienced by souls which have been partly or almost entirely purified in the purgations. It may occur, however, at any point less than the Spiritual Marriage, so that the name is also applicable to the

Thirst of Love.

desire when it is experienced before any purgation has been undergone. The three necessary constituents of the state are, therefore, that some purgation has been undergone (when the thirst is present in one of the higher stages), that some experience of God and the beauty of God has been had, and that during the state some cognition of God is received by the intellect. It is essentially a condition of unsatisfied desire, and therefore may return intermittently until the desire is finally satisfied in God. In strictness the name of Thirst is given only when the desire is continuous and steady : when it is a desire which passes and is gone it is more properly called "Anxiety of Love."

Inasmuch as the state may be experienced by people at very different stages of progress, it has to be remembered that the manner of the Thirst will differ accordingly. In the earlier stages it is accompanied by considerable perturbation and discomfort, which in the higher stages is increased to an almost intolerable pitch of desire, so that it becomes visible in the physical appearance. As in the case of the imperfect Intoxication of Love, some degree of moderation of the Thirst of Love is desirable when it is present in the lower degrees, and an effort should be made to attain a more interior recollection, and if necessary the subject of contemplation should be changed. The natural inclination to proceed to extremities of penance at this time should also be restrained.

The principal effect of this great desire is to render the soul more apt for the reception of divine communications. *Its Effect.*

The Divine Touches belong in reality to the state of Union, and are only given to those who have arrived at that state. They consist of a real but entirely spiritual sensation of God *Divine Touches.*

in the inmost spiritual part, and of the joy of Him, and are evidence of the proximity which characterises the Union. They occur as a rule unexpectedly, very often during conversation, and may be either momentary and very distinct, or more enduring and less clear. It is not possible to describe the sensation which has been experienced, when the moment **Their Effect.** has passed. The effect is an enormous increase of ability and force, which tends to manifest in an active desire to suffer martyrdom for God. The tests for the genuineness of the Touches are therefore : whether the state of Union has been reached; whether the Touches are essentially spiritual, any physical effect being the result of a mere superfluity; and whether the above effects are present. There should be no activity during this state—the desirable attitude is one of passivity and reception, so that the divine communication may not be interrupted.

The state of Mystical Union is Mystical Union in the highest degree of contemplation General. possible in this life, and is therefore the end towards which all the preceding grades of contemplation are directed, and in which they are all perfected. Mystical Union must not be confounded with the union of God with the soul which is the result of sanctifying grace, for that union is dependent on turning from sin to God and not at all on meditation or contemplation, while Mystical Union is never independent of contemplation. The Union does not imply a fusion or transformation as to substance, or a transmutation of essence in the being of God, but consists in acts of cognition and love by means of which the soul is stripped of itself and its own attachments, and is clothed in God and the attachment of God. The Definition. precise definition of it is that it consists in an experimental love of God which is so intimate and close that the soul loses itself utterly in

5

Him; this losing itself meaning here that it loses all feeling and consciousness of itself and its acts, and is aware of nothing but God dwelling within it. It is this loss of the self in God—this cessation of separateness—this transformation into God by love—that is the special mark and the criterion of Mystical Union, for the experimental love of Him may be common to the grades which come before it. The simile of this loss of the consciousness of the self suggested by Richard of St Victor is that of a piece of iron thrown into a very hot fire. It loses by degrees its qualities of blackness and hardness and coldness, and takes on other qualities, which are in effect those of fire. The fact is that it is still iron, but it can easily be conceived as imagining itself to be the fire whose qualities it has taken. This is exactly the case with the soul in the state of Union, which, as St John of the Cross says, "thinks it is God, whereas it is merely a creature."

Disregarding for a moment more the grades of Union, and still treating it generally, it is possible to say that when the soul is united perfectly to God its faculties are in a state of suspension. This amounts to the memory being so immovably fixed in God that any external *species* is unable to disturb it: the fantasy being, as it were, blinded with the great light that shines from God, and unable on its own part to derange the divine action, the intellect being so fixed on God that it can reflect neither on itself nor its actions nor on anything else whatever; and the will effectively lost to itself and changed into God. This complete suspension of all the faculties does not last long without intermission, though the suspension of the will be continuous, but if the total suspension has been interrupted for a time it may often be recommenced.

In spite of the splendour of the Union, it must be remembered that it is not necessary to perfection, for the essence of perfection is simply conformity to the will of God, which is attainable without passing by the way of Mystical Union. This position is rendered necessary by the church's teaching that all states of contemplation are the free gifts of God: the value of the gift of Union is that it promotes with peculiar efficacy precisely this conformity.

The Union cannot, however, be treated effectively as an indivisible whole, for it comprises various grades whose characteristics and variations of intensity must be examined separately. The first of these is the The Simple Simple Union of Love, which is the Union of Love. beginning of the spiritual espousals. In it the faculties are in a state of suspension and are unconscious of their action: the fantasy is, as it were, asleep, the intellect can neither occupy itself with extraneous objects nor reflect on its own acts, and the will is lost to

itself and clothed in God! This loss of
the will, however, is not the absolute
loss of the Beatific Vision, for sufficient
freedom is retained to enable it to
suspend the act of love.[1] With regard
to the faculties, then, the state is
literally that in which it can be said
" I live, yet not I, but Christ liveth in
me." The exterior senses, however,
are not entirely lost, as occurs in
Ecstasy or Rapture, but as no help
is forthcoming from the interior
faculties, there is no comprehension of
any thing seen or heard. A letter or
a word, for example, may be seen, but
it conveys nothing whatever to the
mind. There is a similar inability to
speak or control the movements of the

[1] The text of this passage is as follows : " It
must be noticed that although in this elevation
of the mind the will is not free *quoad speciem
actus* (to use the language of the schools), it is
free *quoad exercitium actus* ; because, inasmuch
as it is not irresistibly rapt in God (as occurs only
in the Beatific Vision), it can suspend the act of
love by its physical power ; and this suffices both
for liberty and merit." Tratt. 3, cap. 17, sec.
160.

body, the explanation being that all the force is concentrated within, and the channels of communication with the external world are therefore inoperative. This incomplete loss of the exterior senses has resulted in the state being also known as an incipient or imperfect Ecstasy.

The Simple Union, then, is a prelude to the Spiritual Marriage, and Its Effects. its effects are such as would be expected from so high a grade. They are not, of course, experienced to the same extent in all cases, nor do they result in their full force from a single experience of the Union, but are produced by a repetition of it, and a gradual acquisition of power. The fervent love for God is accompanied by a vivid desire for complete self-annihilation and surrender to the Divine, so that no place is left for complacent satisfaction with the gifts that have been received. The comparative worthlessness of the self is seen plainly in the light which shines

from God, and the claim of the attrac-
tions of the world is seen to be finally
invalid. As in all states of high adoration, self-immolation appears as a
thing not only to be accepted but to
be acutely desired, and it goes hand
in hand with a fervent energy for
the spiritual welfare of others. The
strength for spiritual activities is
tremendously increased, and the im-
petus towards perfection is so great
that it is impossible to conceal its
effects from the eyes of men. It is a
condition in which the light of sanctity
cannot be hidden, but of necessity
manifests in action.

The above effects, however, are not
in themselves sufficient to prove with
any degree of certainty that the Simple
Union has been reached. The experience of any of the grades of contemplation already described is so
astounding that it will often seem to
the contemplative that he has arrived
at the Union itself, when in reality he
is still in a much lower stage. The

How it may be recognised. Union is as a rule arrived at only after great purgations, and the two marks by which it may be recognised for certain are that, in the first place, all the faculties are lost in God with an incomplete suspension of the exterior senses, in the manner which has been already described, so that what is experienced is a simple intelligence and an experimental love of God, and, in the second, that there is an infallible and ineffaceable certainty that the soul has been with God, and God with it. This conviction is absolute and subject to no doubt whatever; it is not lessened with the passage of time, and is never forgotten: it remains, when all else is uncertain, as the supreme mark of the presence of the Simple Union. But, notwithstanding the exaltation of this grade, it does not imply an absolute security against falling back, and the greatest dangers met with in it are: attachment to anything other than God; carelessness about little things, under the impression that they are unimportant; and an insidious tendency to some measure of self-confidence.

The next grade of the Union is Ecstasy. Ecstasy, a name which has been applied to all cases of total loss of the senses. Strictly speaking, however, these cases are divisible into Ecstasy properly so called, and Rapture, and they will accordingly be dealt with separately. The definition of Ecstasy is that it consists of the Mystical Union of Love in so far as the soul loses the use of its senses completely, without any violence, but rather with a certain calmness. The loss of the use of the senses amounts to a condition in which the eyes see nothing, however obvious it may be; no sound, however loud, is heard; no pain is felt even if the body be burnt or tortured; nothing can be smelt or tasted; and there is a complete inability to move. The necessary functions of the body, such as the circulation of the blood, of course continue, but it appears probable that both the pulse and the respiration are sensibly modified. For the state to be Ecstasy this loss of the senses must result from the Union of Love, and it is suggested that it is directly due to the amazement and adoration and the profound joy experienced by means of the intellect and the will, at the sight of the splendour of God. It is the completeness of the loss which distinguishes this state from that of the Simple Union, and the fact that the loss occurs with great gentleness and no degree of violence that is the point of its distinction from Rapture. During the actual period of the Ecstasy the fantasy and the sensitive appetite are also in a state of suspension, though they recommence their activity the moment that the completeness of the Ecstasy has passed. It must be remembered that the faculties of the soul are by no means suspended: on the contrary, there is no condition in which they are more vividly awake to the things of the Spirit.

The effects of Ecstasy are those Its Effects. of the Simple Union, with so much intensification as is proper to the superior exaltation of the grade.

The existence of Ecstasies in non- Natural Christians necessitates the admission Ecstasy. that such states may be produced by natural means, and not directly by God. The method employed, according to P. Suarez, is that of concentration on some supernatural object, and the result is precisely that the exterior senses lose their power of apprehension. It is probable, however, that the loss is not so complete but that the natural ecstatic would return to his senses if he were subjected to ill-treatment of any kind; and just because the Ecstasy is the work neither of God on the one hand nor the Devil on the other, its effects are as a rule indifferent. It is only in the case of some measure of grace co-operating with the natural effort that some slight benefit may result. Further, a swoon resulting from intense spiritual emotion may sometimes be mistaken for an Ecstasy, and it therefore becomes desirable to discover some tests by which a genuine Ecstasy may be known. It appears that a real ecstatic will always obey a vocal command of his Director, even if that command be that he shall return to a state of normal consciousness; it is virtually necessary that he should have been completely or almost wholly purified by purgation; that the condition with regard to the exterior senses and the spiritual part which has been already described should be fulfilled; and that the effects of the Simple Union should be present in an intensified degree. If these signs are all present there need be no doubt as to the genuineness of the Ecstasy.

How Genuine Ecstasies may be recognised.

Rapture. The general characteristics of Rapture are similar to those of Ecstasy, with the distinguishing fact that in Rapture there is always some element of suddenness and violence in the loss of the senses. The violence is experienced by the intellect and takes the form of some cognition which it cannot reject : the will is never subject to any violence of this kind, for it must remain free. For their better comprehension Raptures are divided Three into three classes, viz. : Classes.

1. Those in which the exterior senses are suspended, while the interior senses (the fantasy and the sensitive appetite) are retained. This is the lowest degree, and is not properly a Rapture at all, because it does not imply Mystical Union with God and has not the characteristic of a suspension of the interior senses. It is a condition which comes about with violence and results in an imaginary vision,[1] the fantasy being flooded with a light which causes all the

1 See Part IV.

attention to be fixed on the object of the vision, and leaves no capacity to receive communications through the exterior senses. It is an intimation received by means of the imagination, the theory being that the recipient is not yet capable of a communication on the plane of pure spirit. In cases where the recipient is patently capable of a more exalted communication, the reason of his experiencing a Rapture which results in an imaginary vision is due to the fact that it is more easily communicable.

2. Those in which both the exterior and interior senses are suspended, and the communication takes place in the intellectual instead of the imaginative part. These are perfect Raptures properly so called, and imply the Mystical Union with God : herein occurs the Betrothal of the soul with God, as an earnest of the Spiritual Marriage ultimately to be celebrated. It is distinguished from that high state by the possibility which

the soul still has of turning back, of breaking off, so to speak, the marriage contract it has signed; the visible apparition of Christ and the gift of a betrothal ring which has occurred with some Saints is at the most a sign of betrothal, already concluded or to be concluded in the future, for that which is a betrothal of spirit with spirit can be celebrated in the spirit alone.

Perfect Raptures are conceded only to those who have passed through all, or nearly all, the purgations, and have been thereby rendered capable of receiving communications in the pure spirit. The suspension of the exterior senses results in the body being apparently dead, and that of the interior senses in there being no power whatever of imagining anything, or experiencing the slightest movement of desire. The soul is, in fact, in a state of high concentration, wherein the only faculties remaining operative are the intellect, which receives the communications by pure cognition, and the will, by which the soul is united to God with the purest and most spiritual love. It is a condition in which all gates are shut, except that which opens into the House of God.

3. Those in which both the exterior and interior senses are suspended in the amazement of the Beatific Vision. This is rarely, if ever, experienced during life, and is not dealt with at present for that reason.

Its Duration. A state of Rapture may last for several hours, or even for several days, but during this period there will be fluctuations in its intensity. At its very highest point—when absolutely all the faculties are centred on the divine object — the duration will scarcely exceed half an hour, but between these highest points there will be intervals during which the will remains immovably fixed, but the intellect and even the fantasy may be concerned with extraneous objects. During such intervals the Rapture may fall to the level described above as the lowest degree of Rapture, with the result that imaginary visions may be seen.

The physical effects in the height Physical Effects. of Rapture are similar to those of Ecstasy: the powers of sight, hearing, taste, and smell are lost, and there is complete insensibility to pain; the respiration is very faint and the body becomes cold. In the intervals the senses are disturbed rather than absolutely lost, and there is no power of distinction between objects presented to them. It is in Rapture that levitation occurs (though it is not of Levitation. itself a proof of Rapture), the body being raised and held suspended in the air; and as this may happen towards the beginning of the state, and before the consciousness has been lost, it is possible for the contemplative to realise what is happening. If there be no levitation the body generally remains in the precise position it occupied when the Rapture commenced, and when the condition has passed

6

the body retains a feeling of health and inexplicable lightness. Cases have also been known in which Rapture has had the effect of curing weakness or ill health.

Spiritual Effects.

The non-physical effects are best considered under the headings of those which are felt during the Rapture, and those which remain when it has passed. In the first place, there is a sensation of intense light and ineffable peace, and the soul receives both imaginary and intellectual visions of the most exalted kind. If they are imaginary they can be to a certain extent explained when the Rapture has passed, but if they are intellectual the very sublimity of their subject renders any description impossible. They are not, however, forgotten, and though their distinctness may fade, they remain always a source of energy and a centre of force in the world of activity. There are, further, flashes of understanding, by means of which the soul is enabled to comprehend in a few moments what years of work would not have sufficed it to learn, and Saint Teresa is so certain of the necessity for these flashes of supernatural illumination that she regards their reception as a sure test of the reality of a Rapture. In the second place, when the Rapture is over, there is a feeling of vagueness and uncertainty as to precisely what is happening, that may last some days, and no kind of assurance as to whether during the Rapture one was in the body or out of it. There is also a tremendous and flaming love for God, and a much more profound contempt than has ever been felt before for the worthlessness of the human part, as a result of the clearness with which its defects are seen in the light of the Rapture. The detachment which is the result of all grades of contemplation assumes so great proportions in the present one, that to all that has been felt previously there is added an actual

physical abhorrence of all that is not
God; and the spiritual strength
acquired is so great that what would
have been an occasion of great danger
even in the Simple Union is here not
only withstood, but transformed into
a means of help and further advance-
ment. The desire to suffer is also intensified, and all the faculties stand ready,
as it were, to answer the call of God.

The
Spiritual
Marriage.
The Spiritual Marriage of the soul
with God is characterised by its
permanence. All previous grades of
contemplation or stages of the Union
are transitory, inasmuch as between
the periods of exaltation the soul
returns to a state wherein the consciousness of the presence of God is
a memory and not a present and abid-
ing fact; whereas in the Spiritual
Marriage the Union is so close and
continuous that the consciousness of
the presence is the normal condition.
It is a perfect and lasting Union in
which there is no question of its

cessation even for a short time, and wherein the soul continually says : " I live, yet not I, but Christ liveth in me." For this reason it is also known as an Habitual Union, as distinguished from the previous stages which are Actual Union, and (by St John of the Cross) as Union of the soul with God after the substance, to distinguish it from all other stages of Union, which he calls Union after the faculties. It is clear from the intimacy of this state that, although the freedom to sin must *Possibility of Sin.* be postulated for the preservation of human liberty, in effect there is no serious question of any sin being committed. Since the man who has reached the Spiritual Marriage is in a great degree still man, he is to that extent in danger of sinning, but since he has the perpetual and unfailing consciousness of God indwelling, sin inevitably becomes for him a moral impossibility. *The Manner of the Spiritual Marriage.*

The particulars of the method in which the Spiritual Marriage comes

about are taken from Saint Teresa, as
being the first contemplative to enter
into details in this connection. God
is regarded as coming down, under
the form of the Trinity, to dwell in the
inmost places of the soul that has
reached this degree—the highest to
which attainment is possible during
life — and thereafter making His
presence known by means of an
intellectual vision of the Trinity
indwelling. This realisation of the
presence of Deity is as of sight, and
no longer as of faith alone, but the
presence is manifested as under a
veil of light, so that the intolerable
splendour of God is not seen face
to face. A clear distinction exists
between the vision of the Union in
the Spiritual Marriage, and all visions
of Ecstasy or Rapture, for in the
Marriage it is clear and distinct,
whereas before it was always to a
certain extent confused and as it were
blind; in the Marriage the Union is
in the centre and substance of the

soul, while in all other degrees it was by means of the faculties alone. The intellectual vision is not regarded as continuous throughout the whole period of the Spiritual Marriage, as this would result in complete incapacity to attend to anything in the outside world, or even to live with one's fellow-creatures; but the consciousness of God indwelling is subject to no change or shadow of vicissitude whatever. It persists, indeed, during all external occupations and disturbances to such a point that there may seem to be some definite division between that part of the personality concerned with the world of sense, and that other part which is unchangeably conscious of God. In the case of Saint Teresa the intellectual vision of the Trinity was followed first by an imaginary vision of Jesus, and then by an intellectual vision of Him which resulted in the soul becoming one and the same thing with God in an intimate union of pure spirit; but, although the Union is always with the Word, the vision of Jesus is not inevitable. It is not mentioned either by Saint Bernard or Saint John of the Cross, and the necessary points of the Spiritual Marriage are, in the first place, the intellectual vision of the Trinity already mentioned, and in the second an intellectual vision of the Divine Word together with some intellectual locution in which a mutual consent is given.

Its Effects. From this incessant consciousness of the indwelling Deity results a degree of peace which no calamity can shake. Though all the universe should thunder in ruin about him, the contemplative who has reached the Spiritual Marriage continues in an interior peace beyond description ; however great the turmoil without, no echo of it can penetrate to the remote depths wherein he communes with God. He is not, it must be remembered, exempt from the difficulties and pain inseparable from existence, but he experiences them rather in the outward part, and in the spiritual part enjoys peace ineffable. Aridity, therefore, is practically non-existent in this state, the kaleidoscopic suggestions of the fantasy are under control, and the passions are finally subjected to the will, for in the possession of the highest good there is little left which may be either hoped or feared. The power of sympathy and the readiness to help remain, but in both cases without any disturbance of the deep tranquillity within. The life of the Christ-Spirit is felt continuously, and not spasmodically as before, with the result that the self and its claims are completely forgotten, and life and death and honour and shame are matters of entire indifference. Perfect conformity to the Divine Will results in an unfailing readiness to suffer any degree of persecution, even to the extent of surrendering all right to eternal salvation if another's spiritual welfare may be helped and the glory of God increased thereby.

Distinct from these effects, there
are also the graces of God that are
received in the Spiritual Marriage.
In a certain closeness of the soul to
God, so intimate as to be spoken of as
a touching of the spiritual parts, the
soul partakes of the perfections of
divinity, and receives the revelation
of the most supreme secrets of God.
A passage from Saint John of the Cross
suggests that the soul by transformation in the Holy Spirit becomes
united and operative with that power
in the Trinity.   A further grace,
conceded only on the very highest

Flame of
Love.

peaks of the Spiritual Marriage, is the
Flame of Love, in which the soul
breaks anew into acts of most perfect
love, kindled thereto by the Holy
Spirit.   In this case the part of the
soul is entirely passive, being re-
stricted to a consent to the divine
action, which operates by presenting
some stupendous truth to the intellect and thereby inflaming the will.
Herein are the supreme heights of the

love and joy of the Spiritual Marriage. Owing to the sublimity of the whole grade it is almost impossible to give any idea of the activities of the soul, but it appears that inasmuch as it feels itself to be one with God by transformation, and to be in fact God by participation, it is able to render to God the gifts of Himself it has received—to give back to Him His perfection and the very Godhead itself —which is the ultimate gift and the only one worthy of acceptance. It is a state in which there exists a continual interchange of the divine gifts between God and the soul, which is the cause of the persistence of the interior peace, and the state itself is in some sense a foretaste of the glories of eternity.

Among the impressions which are received in the Spiritual Marriage, two are singled out for particular mention. The first is a certain hurt of love which occurs in the spirit alone, and has the effect of healing the soul as by burning—it is a touch of the fire of God which heals all ills. It is confined to the Spiritual Marriage, and is the highest degree of that grade, whereas the Wounds of Love properly so called may be experienced outside the grade, and are so in some sense inferior. They have no connection with the pains of purgation, but are caused by a penetrating touch of God which fills the soul with all delight. Their place of origin is then spiritual, though they may also have an effect on the body, and produce actual wounds. In this case the vision of some divine messenger inflicting the wounds in the body is merely symbolical of that which takes place in the spirit, as is exemplified in the case of Saint Francis, and in the case of the wound in Saint Teresa's heart. The interior joy varies in intensity with the physical pain, though if the wounds be only interior and do not affect the body at all, it is of a higher order than when there is a physical

The Wounds of Love. Stigmata.

effect. The tests by which any apparent case of stigmatisation should be proved are: (1) That considerable spiritual progress should have been made, and considerable purgations therefore undergone. (2) That at least some grade of infused contemplation should have been reached. (3) That there should be simultaneously great physical pain and great interior delight. (4) That the pain and the joy should on every occasion of their being felt produce interior recollection and elevation of the mind in God, together with strength in suffering and in mortification.

There is a certain authority for saying that a state very similar to that of Rapture may occur in the Spiritual Marriage, though it is not attended with that suddenness and violence which have been considered characteristic of Rapture properly so called. It is Union in the centre of the soul rather than Union with the faculties, and may take place, accord-

Raptures occurring in this State.

ing to Saint Bernard, with the loss of the senses, though Saint Teresa and Saint John of the Cross consider it to occur without this. In either case it is regarded as a higher state of consciousness than the Rapture which is experienced in the lower degrees of the Union, and does not cause that physical coldness which was characteristic of them. It is a condition in Levitation. which levitation may occur, though without any sensation of the fear experienced in the levitation accompanying the Rapture of the state of Betrothal. This phenomenon cannot properly be regarded as a physical accompaniment of the sp ritual tendency to rise up towards God, because, since God must be regarded as present everywhere, and particularly in the very centre of the soul, a spiritual movement towards Him would result in complete immobility, if it had any physical accompaniment at all. It may be that it is rather a preliminary participation in one of the

characteristics of life after bodily death
—the characteristic, namely, of being
able to move with incomparably less
effort than is necessary in the present
life.

To the question whether the Beatific The Beatific Vision.
Vision, in which God is seen face to
face and without veil, has ever been
conceded to any one in this life, no
full answer need be attempted here,
because even if it be possible it is
inconceivably rare. There are many
authorities on the side of it having
been received by the Virgin, Saint
Paul, and Moses, and as many who
deny that it has ever been enjoyed by
any one except Christ. To the further
question as to whether the grades of
infused contemplation should be de- Should Contemplation be desired and sought?
sired or any effort made to attain
to them, a more detailed answer is
necessary. There is no question that
acquired contemplation may and
should be desired, and attempt made
to obtain it, for its particular char-

acteristic is that its acquisition depends on human effort, with the aid of the ordinary grace of God. In the case of infused contemplation a distinction must be made between desiring it and attempting to obtain it. In spite of some authority to the contrary[1] it is clear that it is both safer and more consonant with humility to hold that human nature is unworthy of so high a grace, and that the desirable position is one of indifference in the hands of God. This is particularly so in the case of Ecstasies, Raptures, Visions, and similar occurrences (with the proviso always that anything may be desired when a divine impulse thereto is felt, as, for example, the Thirst of Love already mentioned), for the very sweetness of the way of infused contemplation makes any desire for it inconsistent with self-sacrifice and humility. Further, it is admitted on all hands

[1] Viz. : Phillippus a SS. Trinitate and Cardinal Lauria.

that infused contemplation is not expedient for everyone, and the utmost that should be done is to prepare for its reception if it should be conceded by God, by making every effort towards perfection, and by continual meditation. For perfection is that which is ultimately desirable, and contemplation, which is the free gift of God, and therefore unobtainable by human effort, is only one means thereto.

IV

VISIONS, LOCUTIONS, AND REVELATIONS

THE grades of contemplation to be treated of in the present section are those in which the comprehension of the divine object is gained with a quality of distinctness and clarity foreign to the grades already dealt with. They are properly grades of *contemplation*, inasmuch as they are accompanied by that fixity of the mind, that sensation of admiration and delight, and that experience of peace which are its essential qualities,[1] but they are definitely a lower and more dangerous variety than those of the previous section, and render the contemplative who receives them more liable to deception. They

[1] See pp. 31, 32 and 41.

cannot be regarded as having any ordered connection, either *inter se* or with the other grades of contemplation, for they are vouchsafed even to those who have made no progress in the contemplative way, and are for this reason considered under a separate heading.

Visions are universally divided into three classes, of which the first is the lowest and the last the highest, viz. : Three Classes of Visions.

1. Corporeal, *i.e.* those which are connected with the exterior sense of physical sight.

2. Imaginary, *i.e.* those which are connected with the interior sense of the fantasy.

3. Intellectual, *i.e.* those which are connected with the spiritual faculty of the intellect.

Corporeal visions, or apparitions, are unexpected manifestations of any object which come about by means of visual *species* transmitted to the eyes, 1. Corporeal Visions.

in a manner different from that of ordinary sight. As a rule the object must be actually present, and in this case the representation is produced by means of divine messengers clothed in aerial bodies — bodies, that is, formed of a combination of air and innumerable elementary particles, representing the object of the vision— and the *species* are then transmitted in the ordinary way; but in some cases the object is represented by means of the mere transmission of the *species* of the object to the eyes without any actual presence of the object. Anything in heaven or earth may be represented in these ways, as, for example, God, Jesus Christ, the Virgin, the dead in any state and the living, the Angels themselves, and Devils. There is no question of the actual physical apparition of these Beings, for the representation is always brought about in one of the ways described, the Devils having the same capacity of taking to themselves

Their
Method.

bodies or transmitting *species* as the Angels.

In the same category as corporeal visions must be placed all other experiences communicated by means of the exterior senses—all music that is heard, that is, and sweet scents, all flavours and sensations of delight—for they are all sent for a common purpose. Physical visitations of all kinds are experienced particularly by beginners, and their chief aim is to lead the recipient towards perfection by the means most natural to his human nature and most suitable to his spiritual immaturity. Since all human cognitions and interior tendencies originate in the exterior senses,[1] the normal method of acting on such tendencies is by the representation to the exterior senses of objects calculated to promote perfection and detachment from the pleasures of the world. It is in reality an adaptation of the divine force to

[1] See p. 25.

the weakness of humanity, and this consideration is applicable to imaginary as well as to corporeal visions, inasmuch as they also are formed in the senses, though in this second case they are interior and not exterior. Corporeal visions being chiefly received by beginners in the way of contemplation, and not having the effect of uniting the soul to God, they are not a sign of any particular sanctity on the part of the recipient, but rather of a want of reaction on his part to the ordinary stimuli ; and the fact that they have also been received by people definitely in a state of sin goes to show that they should not be accounted of too great an importance. At the most they may be a sign of some high degree of sanctity in store for those who see them, who are therefore called upon to make renewed efforts towards perfection.

How True Visions of any kind may be known. The principal signs by which a vision of any kind may be recognised as being of divine origin are :

1. That it causes in the first place considerable perturbation and fear, but that this is immediately followed by a feeling of great joy and peacefulness in the soul.

2. That it is followed by elevation of the mind in God, and a strong disposition to prayer.

3. That it causes deep humility, as a result of the recipient's vivid realisation of his own shortcomings, and a proportionate disinclination to let the vision be known by anyone.

4. That it brings with it a great love of God, as well as detachment and a desire for mortification and penance.

5. That any communication received is both true and of spiritual utility.

It should be particularly noticed in regard to visions of all classes that they should never be desired, both because any such desire is inconsistent with humility and because it opens the door in a particular way to deception. The only proper objects of desire are such things as are conducive

Concerning all Classes of Visions.

to perfection, and the whole array of
visions, locutions, and revelations are
of little value for that, and are in effect
of no great utility in any way, but of
considerable danger. When a vision
of any kind is seen it should first of
all be resisted with all the force possible, for if it be a true vision resistance
will only increase its perfection, and
if it be not of God it will cause it to
disappear. The contemplative should,
in fact, pray fervently that he may not
be led by the way of visions, because
of the great danger of illusion therein
and of the almost insuperable difficulty
he will inevitably experience in avoid-
ing some degree of self-satisfaction ;
but, if persistent prayer have no effect
in preventing the visions, he should
give up all resistance and resign him-
Concerning self to the guidance of God. Where
Corporeal
and the visions are either corporeal or
Imaginary
Visions. imaginary they should be taken in a
spirit of absolute detachment, and be
no more thought of again than if they
had never been received.   The essence

of any such vision lies in the effects which have been mentioned as signs of its genuineness, not in the vision itself, and the good of those effects remains in spite of the complete disregard paid to the actual details of the vision. To this recommendation there are two provisos, viz., that if the memory of the vision persist in returning to the mind without any effort on the part of the contemplative, it should be used as a foundation for more spiritual considerations, and that in cases of aridity the effects may be reflected on for the purpose of arousing spiritual enthusiasm, but the details of the vision must under no circumstances be considered. It is noticeable that during the progress of a vision, even of the most sublime Being, adoration must not be offered until there is no doubt of the vision being divine, and of there being no diabolical deception.

The signs of genuineness and the above general considerations apply 2. Imaginary Visions.

to imaginary as well as to corporeal visions. An imaginary vision is an interior representation of some object, produced in the fantasy by means of *species* either newly combined or newly infused, and in either case illuminated by a supernatural light which causes the object to be perceived with a greater clearness than was possible to physical sight. The vision is produced by a fresh combination of the *species* already present in the fantasy, when it is concerned with matters for which such *species* are adequate, but in cases of particularly sublime visions some new and sufficient *species* must be especially infused, and the imaginary visions brought about in this second way are therefore considered to be of a higher order than those produced by a mere recombination of *species*. The effects of imaginary visions are those of corporeal visions, but, since any imaginary vision is superior to a corporeal vision, the effects are accordingly more pronounced. Their duration is generally very short—the vision is often seen for not more than a flash, and as a rule passes at once into an intellectual vision of the same object. At the first moment both the fantasy and the intellect are fixed on the vision, but almost immediately the concentration of the fantasy is relaxed, the sight therefore disappears, and the whole force is centred on comprehension in the intellectual part. In spite of their brevity, however, the visions leave the *species* of the object so firmly fixed in the mind that it is almost impossible to forget them (except in cases of aridity), and every time they are particularly remembered some measure of their original good effect is reproduced.

In the case of imaginary visions there is an even greater danger of illusion or self-deception than with those that are corporeal, more particularly with imaginative people and women, and it is desirable to have some further tests of their genuineness. The following are, therefore, suggested :

1. That the vision should come unexpectedly, when the contemplative is not thinking about the likelihood of such a thing.

2. That it should be irresistible.

3. That it should not be susceptible of alteration of any kind, whether of addition or subtraction, by the recipient.

4. That it should have the definitely good effects already mentioned.

Intellectual Visions. An intellectual vision consists of a clear and certain apprehension of some object by the intellect, without any form or figure of any kind being seen, and without any actual dependence on the fantasy. It is brought about, similarly to an imaginary vision, by a new combination of the *species* already present in the intellect or by the infusion of a new *species intelligibilis* by God. In both cases the *species* are illuminated by a new and supernatural light, and in neither of them is there any activity of or dependence on the fantasy. The only part, in fact, which the fantasy plays in them is in helping their remembrance. The vision leaves the *species* in the intellect, and some part of the light overflows into the fantasy, with the result that in ordinary cases the fantasy can make enough of the *species* which has been left, by the help of the light it has received, to suffice for memory. Any physical result of the vision is simply a participation by the body in this after-effect on the fantasy. If the object of the vision be, however, very exalted, the pictures of it which the fantasy is capable of forming are so rough and inexact as to give but a very vague representation of the vision itself. In such visions there is no more doubt about the actuality of the "seeing" than if it had been seen with the eyes of the body, and as a matter of fact there is not so much. The object is apprehended with a clearness and absolute conviction that admit of no questioning whatever.

The intellect, it must be remembered, is a spiritual faculty to which God alone has access : the Angels, whether good or bad, are absolutely debarred from entry therein, and illusion by means of a purely intellectual vision is therefore impossible. It may be, as in the former classes, of anything in heaven or earth, and, besides being of God or the Angels or a material object, may be of some truth, divine or human, which is apprehended in itself, as it is, without any mediation of figure or form. A distinction is, however, made in the treatment which should be accorded to intellectual visions of God or the Trinity or the divine attributions or perfections, and visions of created things. In the first case no part of them should be rejected, for they are a great aid to perfection, and instead of being in any way a hindrance to the Union, they are rather a part of it, and never conceded to anyone who is not in some measure united to God. It is, in fact, this which is as a rule the intellectual vision of the Spiritual Marriage, in which the greatness of God is seen with all tranquillity, as well as the Trinity and the interaction of Its Persons, and some further height of splendour which is completely ineffable. But in the second case, where the vision is of something less than God or His attributes, the same distinction should be made as has been suggested in the case of corporeal and imaginary visions. The details, the accidents of the vision, that is, should be rejected once and for all, as far as is possible, with the possible exception of times of aridity, and only the essential effects retained. To regard it as a treasure which is to be stored up in the memory is to be occupied with something that is definitely less than God. Intellectual visions are also divided into two classes according as they are indistinct or distinct, the first class consisting of visions in which the apprehension of the object is absolutely clear and certain, there being no doubt whatever as to its identity, but no apprehension of any details; and the second, of visions in which all the details and qualities are apprehended as clearly as the fact of the vision itself.

The effects of intellectual visions are an intensification of those resulting from the two preceding classes, but their duration may be very different. There have been cases in which they have lasted weeks and months, and rare cases in which they have lasted years, during the whole of which time the apprehension of the object of the vision is present in the intellect. Strictly speaking they are proper to an advanced state of spiritual progress, wherein all or a large amount of the necessary purgation has been undergone, but, as they have also been experienced at considerably less advanced stages, it is impossible to state any definite rule.

There remain two other visions of God, that in which He is seen unveiled and face to face, and that in which He is seen in the Divine Darkness. The first of these is not a matter for consideration in a treatise on contemplation, because it is rarely, if ever, conceded in the present life;[1] the second is that which is spoken of by Dionysius the Areopagite, and should strictly have been treated of in the preceding chapter, inasmuch as it is a grade of contemplation occurring with indistinctness. It is, however, considered here because it is generally known as a vision, and in this connection the distinction drawn between the two methods of knowing God, by affirmation and negation, must be kept in mind.[2]

The intellectual vision of God in Darkness is an intellectual apprehension by means of which the mind, leaving aside all ideas of created

[1] See p. 95.
[2] See p. 36.

things, and abandoning also all
affirmative cognition of God, is
plunged in the incomprehensibility
and unknowableness of the Divine
Essence. This it knows in proportion
to the clearness of its knowledge that
it cannot know, and it is, in effect,
absorbed in the Divine Essence and
lost in adoration. The attitude in
which this incomprehensibility is so
intimately experienced is not one of
cold speculation, but of such an
illumination of the intellect that an
abstract yet stupendous conception
of God is formed, which leaves the
intellect, as it were, in a stupor of
amazement. It is a union with God
Unknown, in which the Darkness is
a Darkness resulting from an excess
of light, and following on this conception is a fervour of love in which the
soul is utterly lost to itself and transformed in God. It is obvious that this
illumination is infused and not acquired, for the very essence of the
vision is that a conception is attained

which is beyond human ability to procure. The characteristics of this vision are, then, that God is known by negation, that the incomprehensibility resulting from this negation is pierced by so high an infused light that it is apprehended intellectually, and that a very abstract but positive and exalted conception of God is formed by which the mind is literally stupefied. It occurs in the grade of Simple Union and at the heights of Ecstasy and Rapture, while the Spiritual Marriage in some cases may be said either to occur in it, or it in the Spiritual Marriage. To a less degree it occurs also in the inferior grades of contemplation, but in such cases the light of incomprehensibility is of a much lower order, and the effects are proportionately less marked. It enters into them, however, in a sufficient degree to explain the lack of distinctness which is a characteristic of all the grades considered in the preceding chapter.

Locutions.   Locutions, which consist of words by which God or His Saints reveal some truth, are of three kinds: Auricular, Imaginary, and Intellectual.

1. Auricular.   In auricular locutions the truth is made known, either by God Himself or by means of angelic intervention, by voices which are heard with the bodily ears in just the same way that a human voice is heard. On some occasions the locution is accompanied by a corporeal vision, and the speaker of the words is seen with the eyes; on others the words are heard without anything at all being seen; but in both cases the voice commands immediate attention and causes a great impulse towards sanctity. These locutions are as a rule received by beginners in the way of contemplation, and should be treated, as regards rejection of the details and retention of the essence, in the same way as corporeal visions.

2. Imaginary.   Imaginary locutions consist of words formed in the fantasy, and though nothing is heard with the bodily ears

the message is received interiorly with a clearness surpassing that of ordinary speech. The words are formed by means of *species* awakened in the fantasy and illuminated with a divine light, so that they are impressed on the sensitive appetite and received by the interior senses in a way similar to that in which the *species* is received by the exterior senses in normal conversation. They may appear to come from a distance, or to resound in the very centre of the heart, and may occur in sleep or while awake and occupied with exterior things, or in prayer. In this last case they are not heard when a Rapture is at its height and the exterior and interior senses are therefore suspended, but in the intervals when some of the faculties, and in particular the imaginative faculty, are free. These locutions are of three kinds, between which there is a real difference, viz., Successive, Formal, and Substantial. Successive imaginary locutions are conceptions

a. Successive.

which the soul, inspired by the Holy Spirit, produces with such readiness that they seem to be actually suggested and spoken by God, when as a matter of fact they are produced by the illuminated intellect and the soul speaks them to itself. This always happens in a state of concentrated prayer, and in absolute strictness they are not properly locutions because they are not received *ab extra*, but unconsciously produced by the intellect. They are to be distinguished from cases in which there is no illumination of the intellect, and the words seem genuinely to be received, though in effect they are the result of a very quick intellectual operation which is purely natural. In the first case the intellect contributes largely in the production of the words ; in the second it produces them entirely, without any divine intervention. The two cases can really be recognised only by their results, for if the words are produced by the natural intellect alone the result is indifferent, with little or no impulse either to good or evil; but if they come from the intellect illuminated by the Divine Light, they cause a definite impulse towards humility and the love of God, as well as a peaceful interior recollection. The course to be pursued in any case is to decrease largely any activity on the part of the intellect, and replace it with acts of love in the will. The probability of the words being produced solely by the intellect is thereby lessened, and the possibility of divine illumination increased.

The second class, which are known b. Formal. as formal, are imaginary locutions proper, in the sense in which they have been described above. They are not always received in prayer, as are successive locutions, and may consist of whole discourses, and not only of a few words. Their purpose is for instruction in the way of perfection, and, besides the actual information they contain, they produce a great readiness to follow whatever instruction is given. There is again a danger that these locutions may be really produced by the person who appears to hear them as coming from without, but such cases are not difficult of recognition. The principal signs are:

Signs of Genuineness.

1. If they are produced there will have been some working of the fantasy and composition of sentences about the object of contemplation; if they are received there will have been nothing except an attitude of attention, and the words will be also more clear and vivid than in the other case.

2. If they are produced they can be hindered, by turning the attention to something else; if they are received they must be heard to the end.

3. If they are produced they can be heard at will; if they are received they can only be heard at the will of God.

4. If they are produced they will have been preceded by close attention to some subject; if they are received

they will be heard quite unexpectedly, and without any previous thought.

5. If they are produced they mean exactly what they say; if they are received they often convey a deeper meaning than appears on the surface of the words.

6. If they are produced and *a fortiori* if they are the result of diabolical deception, they have no good effects; if they are received their good effects are marked.

In any case they should be immediately submitted to the Director, and his advice followed implicitly, even if it contradict the words heard in the locution.

The third subdivision of locutions *c.* Substantial. which are formed in the fantasy is that of substantial locutions, which are vastly more precious than either the successive or the formal. They consist of omnipotent words of God which perform effectively in the soul all that they express. They are clearly heard in the interior of the soul, and are immediately effective in fact—their effect, that is, is not merely to arouse a tendency to any particular course of action. There is here no danger of their being produced by the recipient himself or of their being suggested by diabolical forces, for neither man nor devil is capable of operating to such good effect, but God alone.

3. Intellectual.

Intellectual locutions come about in the manner employed by Angels for communication, without any external voice being heard, or any words in the centre of the soul. The theory of angelic intercourse which holds that they communicate by means of mental concepts directed from one to another must be rejected, because it provides no method by which the attention of the Angel who is being addressed would be aroused. The alternative theory is that one Angel impresses on another the *species intelligibilis* of the concept he wishes to communicate, and to this there are no objections. It is the method employed in intel-

lectual locutions, in which there is
no activity either of the exterior or
interior senses. The *species* of the
concept is impressed on the mind by
God or Christ, or the Virgin (or, in
very rare cases, by an Angel or a Saint),
and the mind receives the concept by
an act of pure understanding, and also
the truth behind the concept. There
is even the possibility of an interchange of thoughts in an intellectual
locution, for the mind can in turn
direct its thoughts to God, and know
that they will be understood. They
may occur either in some high contemplation in combination with an
intellectual vision of God or the
Saviour, or whoever impresses the
species, or without a vision of any kind,
when they take the form of a clear
apprehension of some truth and a
feeling of absolute certainty that it is
from God. In this second case the
locution may frequently be received
without any state of contemplation,
but if this feeling of certainty be lack-

ing the communication is not in any proper sense an intellectual locution, though it may well be a divine illu-

Their Effects. mination.   The locution leaves a sensation of great peace and humility and joy, so that the whole being feels changed and renewed, and the greatest delights of the world are not only undesired but actively disliked, and it is as though a great light had shone in the soul.

Revelations. Revelations in general may be of things both created and divine, as also of things past, or present, or to come. They are an unveiling of hidden truths, or a manifestation of divine secrets, by means of an infused light which imparts absolute certainty of the truth or the secret revealed.   It is not, of course, necessary to the definition that the hidden truth should be universally unknown—the point is that it should be unknown to the particular person to whom it is unveiled, and unknowable by him by any natural means, and so constitute a genuine revelation for him. The apprehension of God and His attributes gained in the state of Union does not fall under the present heading, for it is not essentially a revelation of some absolute secret so much as an elucidation of what was already known by faith.

The principal characteristic of a revelation, or of a prophecy if the revelation is about some future event, is the infused light by means of which the secret is unveiled. It is a light in the intellect, without which no revelation can be held to occur even though all the other points of the definition should be complied with, though it is not a permanent illumination. It flashes out in the mind for a moment to light up the truth or secret to be revealed, and then passes, and the revelation is confined to the particular point seen during that moment. It follows, therefore, that to have received a revelation of one thing does not carry with it a right to speak of any

How they may occur.

other hidden matter; the authority
is limited to the object of the one
particular revelation. It may occur
by means of a corporeal or an imaginary vision, or by an auricular or
imaginary locution, together with the
light of comprehension to understand
their significance; though if it come
by vision the thing seen must be able
to bear a figurative, symbolic, meaning. If no symbolic interpretation is
possible the vision may be perfectly
genuine, but it cannot be regarded
in any way as a revelation. It may
also occur in sleep, when the natural
activity is suspended, and in this case
is effected by a combination of the
species existing in the fantasy of the
sleeper so as to produce symbolic
visions or locutions. A genuine revelation occurring in sleep is, however, very rare, and should be accepted
with great caution owing to the extreme difficulty of correct interpretation. Finally, the revelation may
come about without any locution or

sensible representation whatever, by
the sole means of an intellectual illumination in which the object of the
revelation is seen with perfect clearness. Of all the methods of revelation, the last is the highest, being
more essentially of the spirit, while
revelations occurring in the waking
state are placed above those occurring
in sleep, and revelations by means of
locutions above those received by
vision. Loss of the senses does not
occur when the revelation is by way
of locution, nor when it is by way of
a corporeal vision, for this, as has
been seen, necessitates the use of the
senses. If the vision is imaginary the
senses are necessarily suspended, and
they are also occasionally suspended if
the vision is intellectual, and of an
object which is very exalted.

The purpose of revelation may be Their
Purpose.
either for the illumination and increase
in the love of God of the recipient, and
for enabling him to help others, or
simply for the instruction and help of

observers. In the second case there is strictly no need for any particular sanctity on the part of the recipient, as he is used simply as an instrument, but since a revelation generally requires a considerable amount of interior peace and detachment it is rare for it to be experienced by any one entirely unregenerate, even for the edification of others. It must also be remembered that even in the first case a private revelation is not infallible, and has no force if it be contrary to the direction of the Church.

There is again some danger of a revelation being suggested by the person who appears to receive it, or of its being the result of diabolical Signs of a illusion. The signs by which a true True Revelation. revelation may be known, therefore, are :

I. That it will be true. If, however, it be of a present thing this is not a sufficient ground of belief, but if several *prophetic* revelations have come true it is a ground for believing others.

2. That the object revealed will be indelibly fixed in the memory, and be accompanied by an absolute conviction that the prophecy will come true, however impossible it may seem at the moment.

3. That the recipient of the revelation will disclose everything to his Director, though it will be very difficult for him to speak of it, and will obey the Director implicitly, and that he will further be very unwilling to disclose it to anyone else. These two characteristics are reversed in the case of illusory revelations.

4. That an interior light and restfulness and peace will be experienced.

5. That the revelation will be in strict conformity with the teachings of the Church.

6. That the words of the revelation will be spoken very rapidly, so that an impossible amount will be communicated in a few minutes. The

9

words will also carry with them a much more profound significance than appears on their surface.

7. That the revelation will be useful. It follows as a corollary to this that if they are very frequent they are to be regarded with suspicion.

8. That it will be followed by profound humility.

The value of a revelation, however, even though it be divine, is considerably lessened by the fact that its apparent meaning may not be the real one. In the most perfect revelation the power of correct comprehension accompanies it, but in many others the non-fulfilment of the obvious meaning of the divine prophecy proves that it has been misinterpreted, and that it is in reality only fulfilled in a sense that has not been understood.

The recommendations given in connection with both visions and locutions are to a large extent applicable to revelations generally. Such things, that is, are never to be desired,

for to desire a revelation is to open
the way to deception, and the details
of them should be put aside as soon
and as completely as possible, and
only the essential effect remembered.
The revelations of people in ill-health,
even though this be caused by un-
due mortification, are to be regarded
with considerable suspicion, for such
persons are particularly open to self-
suggestion; and, taken as a whole,
revelations claimed by women should
be accepted less easily than those
claimed by men. This is in spite of
the fact that women are unquestionably more prone to the reception of all
kinds and grades of infused contemplation than men, both by nature and by
the general manner of their life.

V

PURGATION

Purgation Generally. THE grades of contemplation which have been dealt with up to the present are in a certain sense the rewards and delectations of the spirit on its way towards perfection—they are the positive side of a process of which the negative side comes under the heading of purgation. The path of spiritual progress is not simply a passage from one mode and degree of divine consolation to another, but a process in which whatever spiritual sweetness is met with is gained only at the price of a rigorous and searching preparation. There have been cases in which even high degrees of infused contemplation have been reached before any purifying process has been undergone,[1] but

[1] *e.g.* St Teresa.

132

these are very rare in the annals of mysticism and entirely in the nature of exceptions to the general rule. It is not, of course, possible to state any detailed rule as to the manner in which purgations take place, for the process differs with every individual, not only as to the facts of the trial, but also as to its intensity and the time of its duration. It is true, however, in general that progress in contemplation is proportionate to the severity of the purgation. No two cases are exactly alike, but most have some points of similarity, and it is precisely these common factors which make it possible to treat of purgation in general terms. The enquiry must be prefaced by the reminder that not every trouble nor every aridity constitutes a purgation —the ordinary pains and temptations of life must not be magnified to the dimensions of a passive purgation.

Taken in their most general sense, purgations are of two kinds: Active and Passive. Active purgations do *Active Purgations.*

not strictly belong to the Mystic Life,
and will not, therefore, be considered
at any length. They belong properly
to the Ascetic Life, which is a preparation for contemplation, and consist of
all the attempts and efforts made by
the individual, by means of meditation
and the practice of mortification and
control of the senses, to become utterly
detached from all affections which
could hinder him on his way to contemplation. It is a killing out of
affection for everything that is not
God, so that neither country nor
friends nor money nor honour may
stand between the seeker and his end.

Passive
Purga-
tions.
Passive purgations, on the other
hand, consist of those trials and
difficulties which are superadded by
God to the efforts of the individual.
Their aim is equally the purification
of the prospective contemplative, but
they are a purification to a degree
of which he himself is not capable.
They come as bitter aridities and
unlooked-for difficulties and pain,

both interior and exterior, and constitute in effect the refining of the
spiritual gold by fire—and that refining
is a work which is suffered and not
done by the gold itself. Such purgations are themselves of two kinds, the
one being a passive purgation of the Of the
Senses and
senses and the other a passive purga- of the
Spirit.
tion of the spirit. The purgation of
the senses comprises such pain and
trouble of the senses as is sufficient
for the control of the sensitive appetite,
while that of the spirit consists of so
much spiritual suffering as will result
in the conformity of the spirit with
God. The first is for the harmonisation of the senses and the spirit, and
is therefore preparatory to the lower
grades of contemplation; the second
is for the harmonisation of the spirit
and God, and is therefore a preparation
for the grades of Union. Generally,
therefore, the purgation of the senses
is definitely a preparation for spiritual
purgation, but since there is a close
interaction of soul and body some

reflection of the one purgation will always be found in the other, and the trials of the spirit will be aggravated by some trial of the senses, and *vice versa*.

A. Passive Purgation of the Senses.

The Purgation of the Senses. When the first steps are taken in the spiritual life a certain degree of sensible gratification is generally experienced, of which the purpose and the effect are to detach the affections from the ordinary ephemeral pleasures of the world, and attach it to the things which endure. Anyone experiencing this quite naturally tends to the belief that he may flatter himself on the progress he is making, especially when he finds considerable ease in meditation and satisfaction in the practice of austerities; but in effect he has little cause for congratulation, since he has not persevered long enough to make this facility habitual. Its purpose is simply that of promoting detachment from the world, and when

that has been accomplished the consolations and facilities are withdrawn,
and he is left to continue his journey
amidst aridities and pain. It is herein
that he begins to acquire a real virtue,
and at this moment that the purgation of the senses properly begins.
The normal interior condition at the Its Neces-
beginning of this purgation is one in sity.
which a kind of spiritual self-satisfaction is particularly prevalent. The
beginner is inclined to compare his
own apparent progress with that of
others, and remark its great superi-
ority, and accordingly to feel a certain
contempt for their inability to advance.
He is apt to be indignant with their
weakness, and, what is worse, to
resent their receiving any praise from
people whose good opinion he desires,
if by any chance they do succeed in
making some progress. He generally
fails, too, to accept his own shortcomings with reasonable humility, and
apparently bases his disgust on the
idea that so advanced a spirit as his

own should be beyond the ordinary weaknesses of men; while the motive of his application to spiritual exercises is the mercenary one of getting what consolation he can from them. In a word, he cares a great deal more for his own satisfaction and the approbation of himself and his spiritual Directors than he does for uprightness and the light of God, and it is precisely therefore that the purgation is necessary to reduce his monstrous self-conceit. For without the preliminary purification of the purgation of the senses the attainment of any grade of infused contemplation is, except in very rare cases, impossible.

Three Manners of Purgation. The manner of the purgation is best considered under three heads, of which any one or more may be found in any particular case. They are:

1. Aridity.
2. Diabolical assaults.
3. Trouble arising from natural causes, either moral or physical.

Their consideration must be prefaced by a distinction between different classes of devotion, drawn from St Thomas Aquinas. Devotion is of three kinds, viz.:

Substantial devotion, which consists of acts of the will whose purpose is solely the glory of God, without any feeling of consolation at all.

Accidental spiritual devotion, consisting of the consolation and sweetness which is really an accident of the above substantial devotion, but is experienced in the spiritual faculties only.

Accidental sensible devotion, in which the sweetness is again an accident of substantial devotion, but is experienced in the senses, and not only in the spiritual faculties.

1. Aridity is, in the beginning, pre- cisely that sudden inability to meditate that has been already mentioned. The beginner is beyond measure disturbed by it, and flies to the conclusion that he must have been guilty of some very grave sin, and eventually becomes

convinced that he has been abandoned by God. The truth is, however, that this is really the beginning of a very dry and painful contemplation, which is ultimately changed into sweetness and consolation as meditation passes into contemplation. It is caused by the transference of the divine light from the fantasy, in which it gave rise to so much facility in meditation, to the intellect, in which it causes that simple looking to God without discursive thought which is the essence of contemplation. This is, however, unnoticed by the beginner, who is only conscious of the sudden cessation of the light and ease to which he has become accustomed, and is unable to draw any consolation from a light so subtle and delicate as that which has been kindled in the intellect; but, in spite of his being unable to perceive it, it is not therefore inoperative, but has its effect in the perseverance with which he continues his journey towards perfection. The purgation consists, in terms of the distinction which has been drawn with regard to devotion, in a privation of all accidental sensible devotion, though not yet in a privation of accidental spiritual devotion; for it is precisely to the intellect, which is a spiritual faculty, that the illumination is transferred, though of this there is as yet no consciousness.

But all aridities are not necessarily a manner of passive purgation, for they may be caused equally well by a mere lukewarmness on the part of the sufferer or by a natural depression; and Saint John of the Cross[1] gives three signs by which an aridity arising by way of purgation may be distinguished from all others. In the first place, although there be no longer comfort or consolation in the things of God, there will be no tendency to seek them in the things of the world. In itself, however, this is not sufficient, as it might very well result from mere depression, and the second sign is,

The Signs of Aridity being Part of Purgation.

[1] *The Dark Night of the Soul*, Book I, ch. 9.

therefore, that the memory of God is vividly retained, and He is sought in spite of every difficulty. Lastly, the satisfaction and facility which were formerly experienced in meditation will cease, and discursive thought will become practically a matter of impossibility. But, further, although the aridity may be satisfactorily proved to be a mode of purgation, it does not mean that contemplation will inevitably follow. Aridities of a greater or less degree of intensity are the natural accompaniments of close application to prayer, and it has been found that they only point to contemplation when certain conditions are fulfilled. The aridity itself must have been preceded by an unusual degree of consolation —there have been cases in which both corporeal and imaginary visions and locutions have been received by way of foretaste before the purgation began —though the consolations are confined to the interior and exterior senses, and do not extend to the spiritual part.

The Signs of Aridity indicating the Approach of Contemplation.

The aridity must, further, be pro-
tracted, and though in the beginning
it may be interspersed with periods of
consolation, it must finally settle down
into an unrelieved desolation : contemplation, that is, is not indicated if there
are intermittent gleams of light at all
times. Lastly, and this is the principal
sign, it must be practically impossible
to return to meditation when the
aridity is over. If the aridity be
followed by capacity to return to discursive thought, the period of dryness points to nothing further than
perfection in meditation; but if the
return be finally impossible, and this
be accompanied by complete sterility
of all sensible gratification and by a
quiet and simple look of love towards
God, it is a clear indication of ap-
proaching contemplation.

The effects of aridity as a part of the
sensible purgation in particular, and
of that purgation in general, vary, of
course, with the intensity with which
the purgation has been suffered ; but

Effects of Aridity and the Sensible Purgation Generally.

though they differ in degree they are similar in kind. The most obvious result of such an experience is that the spiritual self-satisfaction that was felt formerly is realised to have no kind of foundation, and is therefore replaced by humility. Criticism of others, and indignation at their failings or envy of their success, give place to a conviction of personal unworthiness, and a profound respect and reverence for God take the place of self-congratulation on the consolations that have been received. The consolations, also, are no longer sought for themselves, but the motive of action is purely the love and the fulfilment of the will of God—the mercenary attitude, that is, which preceded the purgation is replaced by one in which the reward is not the motive—for attachment to the delights of the spirit is in no real sense less undesirable than attachment to those of the world. The activity of both these desires is, as a matter of fact, quieted by the purgation of the senses, for the sensitive appetite is effectively crushed, and in the peace which ensues is the beginning of contemplation. It is a condition in which faith is increased, for there is no longer any experience of the objects of faith, hope becomes strong, for it has no earnest of fulfilment but rests on the promises of God, and love for God is proved to be disinterested and sincere, for it is He who sends the trial. In addition, the moral virtues — patience, long suffering, chastity, etc.—are strengthened, but all these effects are true only for those who persist : for those whose energy and courage fail, the purgation of the senses may be the beginning of ruin.

In all considerations of this purgation it has to be remembered that it consists of a privation of accidental *sensible* devotion, and that the spiritual devotion is not affected, but is rather increased by a divine illumination which is the beginning of contem-

General Considerations as to Aridity.

10

plation. The loss of the power of discursive thought, also, is not an absolute inability to form any imagination whatever in prayer, but a condition in which the power of imagining is so obscured that it can only work slowly and, as it were, lazily, without any ability to penetrate below the surface of the object of meditation. When this occurs, it is not desirable to force the mind to do what it is obviously incapable of doing properly. Meditation should be abandoned for the time, and the future contemplative should place himself before God, looking lovingly and intently towards Him in peace and interior quiet, and wait for whatever may occur. There should be no expectation or desire of obtaining any communication, but simply a willingness to await the divine will, for the operation of the spirit is so delicate that the least breath of desire will disturb it. And if this attitude of loving attention before God be impossible, there is no alternative but to be willing to remain in darkness and desolation till the end of life, in conformity with the will of God ; for it must be realised that this is not ultimate abandonment, but transference of the light from the sensible to the spiritual part. Further, though sensible devotion be lost and the real spiritual devotion not yet consciously reached, there is no question but that prayer in some sense is always possible. The will remains free, and with this it is possible to battle through with prayer, though it be apparently empty and cold. But the value of prayer lies in the effort which is made and not in the comfort which is gained, and the prayer that results from a tremendous struggle in the sensible purgation is preferable to all prayers made with ease and consolation.

The second manner of purgation is that of diabolical assaults. This amounts to obsession in the literal sense of being besieged, and is a state 2. Obsession.

less serious than full possession, in which the evil spirit is conceived as entering into the body and the fantasy, and therefrom troubling even the spiritual faculties which it has no power actually to enter. Possession in this full sense is a means of punishment rather than of purgation, and, as it does not in any way make for contemplation, is never included in the methods of purification. Obsession, on the other hand, is a very definite method of purgation before contemplation, consisting as it does in perpetual assaults of one or more spirits of evil, permitted by God to stand, as it were, round the sufferer and assail him with torments and temptations. The spirits are not conceived as entering into the body or the fantasy as conquerors, and have therefore no control over either of them, as is the case in possession, though they may enter in from time to time for the purpose of arousing temptations and causing pain. It is the continuance and ferocity of these assaults which distinguish obsession as a manner of purgation from the normal liability of every man to endure intermittent attacks from the spirit of evil; it becomes, in fact, an habitual condition while the purgation is in progress, and constitutes in effect one of those humiliations which inevitably precede every great exaltation. The details of these assaults are innumerable, and comprise all the catalogue of ills of which the records of Sanctity are full. Visions and sounds of hideous beasts and of the spirits of evil themselves, blasphemies and suggestions of impurity heard in the air, dumbness and inability to eat, incredible sufferings and experiences in the body, unusually violent distractions and inhibitions at time of prayer—in any or all of these ways the obsession may be experienced. They should be met, How it should be if possible, by contempt, and by an withstood. absolute surrender to God with perfect faith in His omnipotence, for of all the means of self-defence resignation is the most effective. Prayer should be continued at all costs, and the suffering itself made the subject of an offering to God, and it has been found that of all the immediate methods of putting the evil spirit to flight, the use of Holy Water is most efficacious. Exorcism is of no avail for any length of time in these cases, though it may afford temporary relief, for the obsession is definitely permitted as a means of purification, and will cease when that has been effected. For similar reasons the advice of ordinary doctors is generally useless, though it is often difficult to decide when the illness is purely natural and when it is part of the purgation. The best test is to notice whether it causes inability to perform spiritual exercises and leaves the patient more or less unaffected at other times, and also to see whether the spiritual remedies, such as Holy Water, are effective or not. If they are, and the spiritual exercises are especially interfered with by the illness, it is safe to conclude that the trouble is due to purgation, in which case ordinary medical advice will be not only useless, but possibly harmful.

But the purgative obsession is not Its Manner. confined to physical difficulties. The most intimate and vital beliefs are assailed by doubts; immortality appears a dream of folly and any conviction of the goodness of God the ultimate irony, while the very fundamental faith in the mere possibility of mystical progress is lost. Hope disappears with the feeling that everything has been lost and God estranged, so that in the abyss of despair suicide appears the only gate of peace. This blackness of despair is the most insidious of all the temptations of purgation, and though it should not lead to the extreme of suicide, it frequently leads to its very brink. There is in particular a temptation to insult and blaspheme all that has hitherto been held most sacred, though at the same time the horror of such behaviour is realised, and it is vividly resented. A violent reaction takes place against all the previous efforts which have been made to gain some degree of self-control, with the result that the passions break out again with renewed energy, and the final touch of horror is added by a sudden increase in the susceptibility of the conscience, so that the normal fear of sinning is tremendously exaggerated. It must be remembered that obsession does not necessarily take all the above forms in any particular case—they are the repertory, rather, from which the trials are chosen—and the best counsel that can be suggested is that some action directly opposed to the particular temptation should be attempted, and that everything should be accepted with resignation and offered to God in sacrifice. To attempt to argue with the spirits of evil is the first step towards surrender.

There remain, as a means of sensible purgation, whatever troubles may
arise through natural causes when
they are especially sent for the purpose
of purification, the natural cause being
simply the channel that has been
chosen, and the purgation working
through it. It may take the form of
illness, or the unexpected loss of
friends or money, whereby a certain
degree of detachment from such things
should be produced in the person
suffering ; or again it may come under
the guise of ill-treatment and persecution. This is its most usual form, and
the sources of the persecution may,
of course, be various. It may come
from enemies or very often from
friends, but it comes in its most
unexpected form when it is suffered
at the hands of admittedly righteous
people. Confessors, Directors, and all
the Servants of God, by misdirection
in spiritual matters, may be used as
the means of persecution, of which
the purpose is finally to root up all

3. Natural
Troubles.

care and interest about personal reputation and honour before men.

Duration
of the
Sensible
Purgation.
The duration of the purgation of the
senses differs, as do all the details
of the contemplative life, with every
individual, so that no probable period
can be indicated during which this
painful purification will be suffered.
There have been cases in which it
lasted for comparatively short periods,
such as two or five years, and others
in which it has extended over as many
as fifteen or twenty.   But whatever
By what it
is followed.
its extent, it is generally followed by
the gift of infused contemplation, and,
as Saint John of the Cross says, by
great liberty and fullness and sweetness of spirit.[1]   The weariness of the
faculties and the tedium of discursive
thought are replaced by the peace of
contemplation, in which there is for
the first time some consciousness of
the illumination of the spiritual part.
It follows naturally that the Thirst of
Love, the passionate desire for God,

[1] *The Dark Night of the Soul*, Book 2, ch. 1.

will be experienced about this time, and that the characteristics of the succeeding grades of contemplation—visions, locutions, even ecstasies and raptures and levitation—will be met with after the cessation of this purgation. Such experiences are, however, generally intermittent, being interrupted from time to time by foretastes of the second and spiritual purgation which has yet to be undergone; and the reception of high spiritual communications at this time is normally attended by some physical discomfort, because the purgation of the senses is not considered to be final and complete in itself, but to be perfected only in the purgation of the spirit.

B. Passive Purgation of the Spirit.

One of the purposes of the second and spiritual purgation is, therefore, finally to cleanse the sensitive part from all its remaining imperfections, and to root out utterly the defects that have already been brought under

The Purgation of the Spirit. Its Purpose.

control. A further purpose is the cleansing of the spiritual part, which has been virtually untouched by the sensible purgation, for neither Simple nor Perfect Union (to both of which the second purgation is preliminary) are possible while any of these imperfections remain. There is still a tendency for the mind to wander from a strict attention to God and to concern itself with creation rather than the Creator, as well as some degree of blindness which results in a liability to deception in the matter of visions and locutions, and a confidence in them which they do not merit. These are more particularly defects on the part of the intellect, but the will also is in need of further purification. A certain measure of attachment to the graces and consolations of God remains, accompanied by sufficient self-love to cause self-satisfaction about their reception, and detachment even from divine consolations must be attained before the

Union is possible. Finally, the tendency to act in accordance with the natural inclinations of the faculties must be replaced by complete conformity with the will of God, for without this the divine action necessary to the Union will be rendered impossible.

On the face of it, it seems impossible to imagine anything worse than the pains of the first purgation, but those of the purgation of the spirit are beyond comparison more appalling. It is a condition in which the soul seems to dissolve in the atrocity of its distress, from which death would be a merciful release, for the suffering can only fitly be compared with the pain of Purgatory and Hell. It follows, as a rule, the consolations which succeed the first purgation, though in rare cases [1] both purgations may be suffered simultaneously: but it must be remembered that just because the number of souls arriving at the state of Union is small compared

The Time of its Occurrence.

[1] *e.g.*, Angela of Foligno.

with the number which arrive at the lower grades of infused contemplation, so the number which undergo the spiritual purgation, which is preparatory to the Union, is smaller than the number which pass through the purgation of the senses, which is precedent to those lower grades.

The Manners of the Purgation.

The manner in which the purgation of the spirit is experienced is, in the first place, by spiritual aridity. This is a privation of all accidental spiritual devotion,[1] so that, while the substantial devotion continues in full force, there is yet no consciousness of it either in the spirit or the senses. The essential part of devotion remains, that is, so that the readiness for sacrifice and the great love of God persist; but as no reflection of this finds its way into the spirit or the senses, the only sensation is one of

Purgative Illumination.

tedium and emptiness. This is not in itself, however, a purgation of sufficient severity for the attainment

[1] See p. 139.

of Perfect Union, which necessitates
a further purification by means of a
light of high contemplation, which at
first, by its very brilliance shining on
the imperfections of the soul, ob-
scures and hurts it in all its parts,
but later, when the purification has
been accomplished and the imperfections removed, becomes the illumination of the Perfect Union with God.
It may take a slightly different form, Another
as with Saint Teresa, and appear as a Form.
light of contemplation in which there
is a momentary experience of God,
to be followed instantly by the realisation of His infinite farness. It is not
a process of the fantasy, but an effect
of the purgative illumination in the
intellect, and constitutes a Wound of Wound of
Love of a different kind from those Love.
mentioned in connection with the
Spiritual Marriage. Its effect is
entirely spiritual, and the agony of
the separation is so great that to the
sufferer it seems that death must
follow immediately. Strictly it is only

known as a Wound of Love when it is felt suddenly, the name of Faintness or Languor of Love being used for the same experience when it approaches gradually. The purgation in both cases consists of the unfulfilled longing aroused by such a sight— Saint Teresa's own expression is that the soul is crucified between heaven and earth—though in the Wound of Love it is accompanied, strangely enough, by a certain sweetness and love. In this case again the illumination is that by which the Perfect Union is ultimately accomplished, and from this last fact it results that in the ordinary course the Perfect Union will follow such purgations, for the soul is already in possession of the light essential to that state.

The illumination constituting this second manner of spiritual purgation, whatever form it may take, is the Divine Darkness of Dionysius the Areopagite, and appears to the contemplative as darkness because of its own purity and brilliance and his imperfect capacity to receive it. It is so bright that it blinds him, and this darkness extends to all parts of his personality. Its effect on the intellect has been seen in the blindness in which nothing can be clearly perceived, and the will is afflicted by total inability to contemplate anything but the hideous imperfections of the soul. They stand out with a new and amazing clearness in the light of the divine illumination, and result in a conviction of absolute abandonment by God. The memory is unable to contribute any comfort, for all remembrance which might afford consolation is blotted out, and only the memory of pain and agony remains. Even the recollection of divine consolations in the past only serves to aggravate the condition in the present, for it is accompanied by a feeling of certainty that they will never be experienced again. The pain, it is seen, originates in the spiritual faculties, but all its

Effects of the Illumination.

II

agonising effects are felt to their full in the sensitive appetite. In addition to the actual distress of the faculties, they are in a sense bound, and unable to fulfil their ordinary duties. Both the intellect and the will are so closely concerned with their own imperfections that the one is incapable of any contemplation of the things of heaven, and the other can concern itself neither with the things of heaven nor those of earth, except in both cases in a manner so dry and difficult as to suffice for the vindication of freedom, and not for any comfort or consolation. The memory is in a worse condition still, for the recollection of its own defects so engrosses it that it is quite incapable of attending to anything else, and has long fits of absolute blankness, while the sensitive appetite feels no kind of enthusiasm either for God or any part of creation. In a word, it is to all intents and purposes a

Duration of the Spiritual Purgation.

condition of abject hopelessness which precedes a fulfilment beyond all hope, and, though there is no universal rule, it generally continues for some years. There are in many cases intervals which serve for recuperation, in which it is occasionally felt that the trials are finally over. They are foretastes of the real and positive purpose of the illumination, but where they occur the spiritual purgation is spread over a longer period than in the cases where there is no break, until the purification has been fully accomplished.

The effect of this stupendous trial Its Effects. is to purify the soul from precisely those imperfections which were mentioned as persisting after the sensible purgation had been completed, and to enable the contemplative to abandon himself, indifferent and destitute, into the hands of God, as clay in the hands of a potter.

During the progress of the purga- The Burning of Love. tion, and in proportion as the purification proceeds, the flames of love for God which burn without ceasing in the substance of the soul, even during the most tremendous desolation, begin to make themselves felt in the part in which the soul is conscious. It is a penetration into the realm of consciousness of that which has continued, unnoticed yet without a break, in the will — the pure substantial devotion combines again with some measure of accidental spiritual devotion, and with this accidental devotion the fire of longing fills all the activities of the soul with a passion of desire for God. The need for God fills every thought and is present in every action, so that there is no peace or satisfaction until He is found. The soul is pictured as touched with the realisation of this desire at a moment when it is at the very depth of dryness and spoliation, and the violence and energy with which it responds are a natural result of the sterility in which it resided; it is as though a flash of divine light broke through the darkness of self-disgust, and the desire leaps up in a frenzy of hope renewed. And when the purga-

tion draws towards its appointed end
and the intellect has been greatly
purified among the shadows of its
desolation, there is felt in that faculty
a foretaste, or rather a beginning, of
the divine union to which the purgation
leads, and the sweet savour of God is
experienced in a peaceful and quiet
illumination. In this connection it
should be noticed that the intellectual
illumination is preceded by the re-
awakening of love and desire in the
conscious part, and that the periods
of elevation are intermittent only—
periods, as it were, when the curtain
of suffering is raised, and the soul
becomes momentarily conscious of
the work of preparation that is being
carried out. Such periods must, of
course, be received with a due detachment, for a too great anxiety in their
respect will only produce bonds of
attachment which will be in their turn
the subject of further purgation. The
desire, moreover, and the infused love
for God which are felt, are not a mere

repetition of the desires experienced at the completion of the sensible purgation, for those were of the senses, but these are of the spirit demanding a spiritual fulfilment.

The Signs of Suffering being part of the Purgation.

Just as in the case of the former purgation so in the present one, all pain and distress must not be taken as constituting the spiritual purification. It is indicated in general only when certain conditions are fulfilled, of which the chief are :

1. That the suffering has been preceded by the purgation of the senses, and the illuminative state consequent thereon. This condition obviously need not be satisfied in the rare cases where the two purgations occur simultaneously.

2. That the soul is so deeply concerned about its own imperfections that it is incapable of meditation or contemplation, and as a consequence experiences such a degree of spiritual distress as very nearly results in death. It goes without saying that

this distress must be caused by the fear of having offended God, and the fear and conviction of having been abandoned by Him.

3. That in spite of this fear and dejection there is so strong a love for God that any suffering would be undertaken for His sake, and any possible thing done rather than offend Him.

4. That physical pain and the persecutions of men are so outweighed by the interior suffering that the edge of their intensity is to a large extent blunted.

5. That during the progress of the purgation the flame of spiritual love and desire already mentioned is experienced.

In spite of the inexpressibly greater horror of the second purgation, it is nevertheless a less dangerous condition to be in, if it be supported with willingness and resignation, than the purgation of the senses, for throughout the whole period the infused love for

The Spiritual Purgation less dangerous than the Purgation of the Senses.

God both strengthens and supports the soul, although there may be no conscious knowledge of this. It is an advantage, too, that the faculties, both rational and sensitive, should be bound, for inasmuch as all evil arises from a misuse of the faculties, the probability of definite sin is lessened by their being rendered largely inoperative. For the darkness in which they function results not from a loss of light, but from so great an increase and fullness of illumination that they are virtually blinded by it, although in that very light they are nearer God and His protection. The final safeguard is that the progress in the second purgation is a progress in suffering which is the greater and the more acute for being spiritual, and is therefore of more efficacy for the thorough purification which in the ultimate event makes the soul one and the same thing with God.

INDEX

Visions, 45, 142, 155–6.
  corporeal, 99, 116, 126.
    how produced, 100.
    how to be received, 104.
    purpose of, 101.
    subject of, 100.
  imaginary, 99, 126.
    duration of, 107.
    how produced, 106.
    how to be received, 104.
    in Rapture, 77, 82.
    in Spiritual Marriage, 87.
    signs of genuineness of, 108.
  intellectual, 41, 99, 123.
    distinct and indistinct, 111.
    duration of, 112.
    how produced, 108.
    how to be received, 110–1.
    illusion impossible in, 110.
    in Rapture, 82, 86.
    in Spiritual Marriage, 86–8, 111.
    of the Trinity indwelling, 86, 90.
    subject of, 110.
  not to be desired, 103.
  signs of divine origin of, 102.
  to be resisted, 104.

Will, 17, 23, 27, 156.
  difference of, from sensitive appetite, 24.
  during purgation, 164.
  in perfect Intoxication, 57.
  in Prayer of Quiet, 51–2, 54.
  in Prayer of Recollection, 46.
  in purgative illumination, 161–2.
  in Rapture, 80.
  in Spiritual Silence, 49.
  in Spiritual Sleep, 59, 60.
  in Union of Love, 68–9.
Wound of Love, 159–60, and see Stigmata.